The Essays

of

Henry Timrod

The Essays

of

Henry Timrod

Edited with an Introduction by

EDD WINFIELD PARKS

1942
The University of Georgia Press
Athens

Paperback edition, 2007
© 1942 by the University of Georgia Press
Athens, Georgia 30602
www.ugapress.org
Designed by Paul Perles
Printed digitally in the United States of America

The Library of Congress has cataloged
the hardcover edition of this book as follows:
Library of Congress Cataloging-in-Publication Data

Timrod, Henry, 1828–1867.
The essays of Henry Timrod, edited with an introduction
by Edd Winfield Parks.
vi p., 2 L., 3-184 p. 23 cm.
1. Poetics. I. Parks, Edd Winfield, 1906–1968, ed.
PS3071 .P3   814.3
(OCoLC)924212   42-18682

Paperback ISBN-13: 978-0-8203-3146-1
ISBN-10: 0-8203-3146-5

Preface

‖‖‖

A POET's prose frequently has a double value. It may have an inherent distinction, and it may help to explain and round out his poetry. When his prose is mainly concerned with the theory and practice of his craft, or with the background of life out of which his own verse is written, the poet speaks with an unusual authority. He is giving explicitly what otherwise is only implicit in his work.

This is true of Timrod's essays. In them, Timrod becomes the analyst, the debater, the man at once attacking and defending: he ceases to be the artist, that he may talk about the principles of his art. His talk is vigorous and interesting, if not completely valid. There are blind spots which he did not recognize; in compensation, there are the opinions that came from long thought and quick moments of insight.

I have re-published all of Timrod's essays, and in the notes all of his identified editorials that deal with literature. Three essays are reprinted from *Russell's Magazine;* the fourth, "A Theory of Poetry," from Timrod's manuscript. Since in one essay he was directly answering William J. Grayson's little-known essay, "What is Poetry?", I have added this in an appendix. In the Introduction, I have levied freely on Timrod's letters, published and unpublished, wherever they add to his critical thought or illustrate his reading.

The preparation and publication of this book was made possible by a grant-in-aid from the University Center of Georgia, and by the co-operation of the officials of the University of Georgia. For permission to use unpublished letters, and Timrod's copy of "A Theory of Poetry," I am indebted to Miss Ellen Fitz-simmons and the Charleston Library Society; for unpublished letters and passages from the unpublished autobiography of William J. Grayson, to Professor R. L. Meriwether and the South Caroliniana Library of the University of South Carolina; for Timrod's letters to Rachel Lyons, to Professor William Fidler and the University of Alabama Library. The Timrod material in the Paul Hamilton Hayne Collection at Duke University has recently been published by Professor Jay B. Hubbell in *The Last Years of Henry Timrod*. It is pleasant to record a specific indebtedness for the use of excerpts from the letters in that book, and a general one to Professor Hubbell for his aid. I have used a few items from Professor Guy Cardwell's *The Uncollected Poems of Henry Timrod*. Mr. Marshall Uzzell read the manuscript, and made several valuable suggestions. In addition, I have been greatly helped in preparing this book by the staffs of the University of Georgia Library, University of North Carolina Library, Duke University Library, Library of the College of Charleston, the Library of Congress, and the New York Public Library; by Mrs. Brainard Cheney of the Vanderbilt University Library and Mrs. Minna C. Martin of the Emory University Library; and by Mrs. Henry D. Holmes. In all of the work I have had the generous and intelligent co-operation of my wife, Aileen Wells Parks.

E. W. P.

Contents

‖‖‖‖‖‖‖‖‖‖‖‖‖‖‖‖‖‖‖‖‖‖‖‖‖‖‖‖‖‖‖‖‖‖‖‖‖

PREFACE   v

INTRODUCTION   3

THE CHARACTER AND SCOPE OF THE SONNET   61

WHAT IS POETRY?   69

LITERATURE IN THE SOUTH   83

A THEORY OF POETRY   103

APPENDIX: William J. Grayson "What is Poetry?"   135

NOTES   157

INDEX   177

The Essays

of

Henry Timrod

Introduction

TIMROD AS CRITIC

TIMROD'S prose and verse are closely related. They reveal the same intense, disciplined mind, the narrow range of interests, and a constant preoccupation with aesthetic and ethical and strictly poetic problems. Much of his early criticism was cast in verse; with one exception, his essays discuss the ontology of poetry. Although he worked as tutor and newspaper editor during most of his adult life, these jobs were a means to living. His justification, his reason for being, was in his poetry. Even in the harshest days of war and reconstruction, of poverty and illness, he continued to write: his best poem is a product of these years.

The war gave depth to his thought, intensity to his feelings. His note of melancholy was wrenched into the deeper, more abiding note of tragedy. The poems become dramatic contrasts. He retained his earlier concepts of nature and mind and soul; against these he set the blood and hatred of war. He found his individual theme late in his short life and he wrote only a few poems on it; but his earlier verse and his critical ideas combined to give him the technical equipment needed for an authentic final achievement.

Timrod made three formal attempts to define the nature

3

of poetry. Indirectly through other poems, essays, and editorials he revealed in glancing allusions or brief, considered statements his pre-occupation with this problem. His basic ideas did not change. The later presentations do not contradict the earlier; rather, they show the full development of his thought, and the final form of a tenable, rounded aesthetic of poetry.

A protecting cloak of fiction and of poetic convention is thrown around his first attempt. "A Vision of Poesy" [1] is cast in verse; the protagonist is an anonymous fictional character. But the sentiments spoken by him and to him are the beliefs of Henry Timrod; in thought, although not in fact, the work is autobiographical.

"A Vision of Poesy" is the product of youth; it is, Hayne notes, marred "by a too evident lack of harmony and unity of parts, proceeding from the fact that the narrative was composed in sections, and after the lapse of periods so long between the different *bouts* of composition, that much of the original fervor of both conception and execution must have evaporated." [2] The underlying concept is clear enough. Timrod is presenting the subjective sources of poetry; or, in Hayne's phrase, "the true laws which underlie and determine the noblest uses of the poetical faculty."

The protagonist as a youth had more than ordinary sensibility. Strange portents had marked his birth; afterward, the child had seemed withdrawn, and frightened his parents by a strange far look and by "brief snatches of mysterious rhymes." [3] He is conscious of uncomprehended mysteries,

---

[1] *Poems of Henry Timrod* (Memorial Edition, with memoir by J. P. K. Bryan; Boston, 1899, and Richmond, 1901), 74-100. Later references to this book will be to: Timrod, *Poems*.

[2] Paul Hamilton Hayne (ed.), *The Poems of Henry Timrod* (New York, new revised edition, 1872), 30-31.

[3] Timrod, *Poems*, 75.

of an intuitive understanding which he can not order with thought, and of strange emanations from natural phenomena. He is troubled by dreams and disturbed by thoughts that alike elude his grasp. One night when he has gone in solitude to a favorite nook deep in the woods, a spirit appears to him—or seems to appear. She is the angel of Poesy, and she reveals the high mission of the true poet.

The task of Poesy is closely related to that of religion, though definitely subordinate to this "mightier Power." She helps to keep the world spiritually "forever fresh and young"; [4] to arouse in men the nobler emotions and desires; to "turn life's tasteless waters into wine"; and to inspire poets to seek as much knowledge as men can learn, and to translate that knowledge so that ordinary men can understand it. But Poesy can only "sow the germ which buds in human art." The poet himself determines the result. If he is, as poet, worthy, he must be pure and consecrated; he must belong "to the whole wide world." Timrod deliberately reverses the famous statement of Keats on beauty and truth: the poet must be "assured that Truth alone / Is Beauty." Mindful of this, he sings not merely for himself, or of his own subjective thoughts and longings; he sings for those who grope and wonder, and can not sing.

Timrod breaks off the fable to comment directly on the inability of the poet to present his full concept. The idea had seemed alive "to the Poet's hope within my heart," but as it became an actuality, the concept lost its semblance of life.[5]

The third section of "A Vision of Poesy" describes a man grown old while yet in the prime of life, a poet who has

---

[4] *Ibid.*, 85. The following quotations in this paragraph are from pages 85-90.

[5] *Ibid.*, 90-92. Quotation on 91.

largely failed because, misunderstanding the sources of art, he has yielded to a morbid subjectivity. This concern with self, partly brought on by the scorn of the world and by the disdain of the woman he loved, had vitiated his poetic accomplishment. He returns home to die. But the angel of Poesy appears to console him. Although the fault of hidden selfishness had marred his verse, he had been scornful of specious falsehood, and he had uttered "Truths that for man might else have slumbered long." This ingrown morbidity had prevented his attaining full stature, for the great poet "spheres worlds in himself." He must be concerned with the mysteries of his own soul and mind, but "on the surface of his song these lie / As shadows, not as darkness": he makes use of the personal light to help clarify the general darkness.[6]

Timrod points the contrast between partial achievement and completeness. A complete poem is an ethical poem; it not only functions within itself, it acts upon the world to make for positive good. His terms are romantic, and his words often abstract. As a poem, "A Vision of Poesy" is uneven, frequently unconvincing, and at best achieves only a limited success. As a vehicle for his critical theories, it is less persuasive than his essay, "A Theory of Poetry."

Several writers have suggested that Timrod in this poem was greatly influenced by Shelley's "Alastor."[7] Since Timrod's immature work seems a beginning yet also an integral part of his critical theory, and is so treated here, it is useful to compare the two poems.

Both Shelley and Timrod write of an idealistic young poet

[6] *Ibid.*, 92-100. Quotations 98-99.
[7] To cite one old and one very recent example: G. A. Wauchope, *Henry Timrod: Man and Poet* (Bulletin of the University of South Carolina, 1915), 22, and G. A. Cardwell, Jr., *The Uncollected Poems of Henry Timrod* (Athens, Georgia, 1942), 4.

who finds tragedy rather than a fulfillment of genius; in each poem, the young man broods in solitude upon the majesty and mystery of nature. The resemblances are circumstantial, not spiritual. Alastor is essentially Shelleyan, or Byronic. He is dedicated to poetry, to earth, to nature. But in his quest of the spirit of poetry he left an "alienated home, / To seek strange truths in undiscovered lands"; he has pursued "Nature's most secret steps" in strange and far-off places, and in the "awful ruins of the days of old." [8] It is essentially a traveler's concept of nature, not a mystic's; the revelation that he could never hope to find at home might somehow come to him in Arabia or Ethiopia or the Arctic. Although Shelley states the opposite, Alastor apparently seeks understanding through experience, not through contemplation. Timrod's young poet has an entirely different concept of nature. He is more Wordsworthian than Shelleyan, although he lacks Wordsworth's certitude and spiritual rapport with nature. It is the Wordsworthian mystical comprehension that he seeks. For that, he goes deep into the woods and takes as teachers the leaves, the trees, the stars, the sky, and the wind. He depends upon intuitive reverie, rapt contemplation, and revelation; [9] he seeks them in the familiar solitude of his own region instead of in the wanderings of Alastor.

Each poem uses a dream symbol. But Alastor's is a simple dream of a maid who typifies the spirit of poesy. Her voice "was like the voice of his own soul." She represents the unattainable perfection that he yearned for.[10] She is an oriental goddess or houri for whom Alastor feels a physical as well as

[8] *The Poetical Works of Percy Bysshe Shelley* (edited by Mrs. Shelley; Boston, 1881), I. Above quotations, 162-63.

[9] Timrod, *Poems*, 75-76, 81-85.

[10] Shelley, *op. cit.*, 164-66. Following quotation, 163.

mental passion; having known her in a dream, he can never be satisfied with the earthly love that a woman can give. His wanderings become wilder, more frantic: seemingly, the ideal unattainable in life might somehow be attained in death. The anonymous poet in "A Vision of Poesy" does not have the sensation of "shuddering limbs and . . . gasping breath;" he is not, in fact, quite certain whether he has in his solitude dreamed of a maiden, or been visited by a spirit: " 'Here was it that I saw, or dreamed I saw, / I know not which, that shape of love and light.' " [11]

However briefly, Alastor possessed the maid who personified poetry; in Timrod's vision, Poesy remains aloof and remote. She will not give the young poet full knowledge of the mysteries, but only so much as a mortal can know. Even then, she limits her promise severely. She gives the fire and genius, but the "true bard is his own only Fate." [12] The poet fails in Timrod's version through his own human faults, and not through a vain quest after the unattainable. He too has known solitude, brought on him by the scorn of a material world and the scorn of a beautiful woman. But Poesy, while she comforts him, places the blame directly on him; he has grown too enwrapped in his own thoughts, and heeded too little the cares and aspirations of other people.

Timrod's concept of the ideal has little relation to Shelley's. Alastor sought a perfection that had, except in the strikingly physical personification of poesy as a woman, no concern with the things or people of this world; he sought it by romantic, concretely geographical wanderings. In his Preface, Shelley notes that "The Poet's self-centred seclusion was avenged by the furies of an irresistible passion

[11] Timrod, *Poems*, 93.
[12] *Ibid.*, 85, 88.

pursuing him to speedy ruin." [13] But Alastor is self-centered before his dream, as well as afterward; and the dream itself encourages this egoism and leads him to destruction. Timrod's poet fails, at least in part, because he forgets or ignores the nobility of his vision. He has had his moments of insight and of accomplishment. He has been "A priest, and not a victim at the shrine." [14] His work has had positive value; it leads to loneliness and sorrow, but not to ruin.

In death, as in life, these imaginary poets present basic differences that are more important than their superficial resemblances. Shelley set out to write an allegorical tragedy; Timrod sought to give meaning to a poet's life through a complex vision. Even the machinery and forms of the poems differ. Timrod may have found in "Alastor" a suggestion that kindled his poetic imagination; but Timrod's philosophy was too far removed from Shelley's for this suggestion to do more than start him on his own way.

In other respects, Timrod's resemblance to Shelley is slight.[15] Each believed in the nobility and the mystical power of poetry; each man was integrally a part of the romantic movement. Timrod had read Shelley's "A Defence of Poetry," and twice he quotes approvingly, but inaccurately, the definition of poetry as "the record of the best and

[13] Shelley, *op. cit.*, 157-58.

[14] Timrod, *Poems*, 99.

[15] Several critics have thought they detected a stronger influence than I can find. Peirce Bruns (in the *Conservative Review*, I: 263-77, May, 1859, p. 268) makes by far the strongest statement that I have seen; he thinks there is little resemblance between Wordsworth's handling of nature, and Timrod's: "Timrod, in this regard, at least, is far nearer to Shelley." Walter Hines Page (in the *South-Atlantic*, I: 359-67, March, 1878, p. 365) says that two or three stanzas of "A Summer Shower" remind him by their exquisite movement and beautiful fancy of Shelley's "Cloud." Jay B. Hubbell (*The Last Years of Henry Timrod*, Durham, 1941, p. 127) suggests that Timrod's "Song" (first line: "The Zephyr that toys with thy curls") is "reminiscent of Shelley's 'Love's Philosophy.'"

happiest moments of the happiest and best minds." [16] These
words had impressed Timrod as truth; he was in full agree-
ment. But the extent of his disagreement with Shelley's ideas
is most apparent in their respective treatment of inspiration.
In the paragraph preceding his definition, Shelley had identified poetry as something divine, and the poem as super-
nally inspired: "I appeal to the greatest poets of the present
day, whether it is not an error to assert that the finest
passages of poetry are produced by labour and study. The
toil and the delay recommended by critics can be justly
interpreted to mean no more than a careful observation of
the inspired moments, and an artificial connexion of the
spaces between their suggestions by the intertexture of conventional expressions." [17]

Without mentioning Shelley's words and probably without considering them worth a rejoinder, Timrod contra-
dicts this theory of art. He insists on making a clean and
sharp distinction between the subjective essence of poetry
and the objective, tangible poem.[18] This distinction governs
his treatment of inspiration. He felt that a poet's mind had
to be stimulated, roused, inspired. The stimulation might
come from within, through a chance day-dream or dazzling
thought; it might come after long contemplation of some
natural or human phenomenon; the spark might be kindled
by some external pretty face or casual word. In his college
days, "Every pretty girl's face acted upon me like an inspiration;" [19] in his greatest poetry, the tragedy of war

[16] In "What is Poetry?" and "A Theory of Poetry."

[17] Shelley, "A Defence of Poetry."

[18] In varying forms, this distinction appears in three of Timrod's essays:
"The Character and Scope of the Sonnet," "What is Poetry?", and "A
Theory of Poetry." For a good, brief discussion of his essays, see G. P.
Voigt, "Timrod's Essays in Literary Criticism," in *American Literature*,
VI: 163-67, May, 1934.

[19] Hayne, *op. cit.*, 19.

served as a more powerful stimulus. But this inspiration, whatever its cause, acted upon the mind of the poet, taking hold of his imagination or being played upon by his fancy. There was a mystical quality involved; the poet differed from the ordinary man principally in his being able to express this inspiration: "The ground of the poetic character is more than ordinary sensibility." [20]

When he presented his idea of inspiration through the objectifying medium of poetry, Timrod emphasized the mystical concept. His youthful poet not only gets a sense of mystery from the trees, skies, and winds, he also murmurs rhymes which he does not himself understand, and feels dull, clinging memories of a mystic tongue and a once-clear comprehension.[21] Inspiration, embodied in the form of the angel of Poesy, rouses, troubles, and perplexes his soul, and drives his mind on to such knowledge as mortals can attain; she is the light of the poetic imagination. Yet even in this romantic concept, Timrod allows to inspiration only the function of beginning the poetic process. The poet's reach depends upon himself. He alone can govern his poem, and he must do it through his own knowledge and technique.[22]

When he spoke more prosaically, in his own person, Timrod shied away from defining inspiration. He knew, for himself, that it existed, but he knew also that it had limits. In trying to prove that the sonnet was no more artificial than other forms of verse, he stated flatly that "If the poet have his hour of inspiration (though we are so sick of the cant of which this word has been the fruitful source, that we dislike to use it) it is not during the act of composition. A distinction must be made between the moment when the

[20] Timrod, "What is Poetry?"
[21] Timrod, "A Vision of Poesy," *Poems*, 75.
[22] *Ibid.*, 85-88.

great thought first breaks upon the mind . . . and the hour of patient and elaborate execution. It is in the conception only that the poet is the *vates*. In the labor of putting that conception into words, he is simply the artist." [23] Otherwise, the poet would be merely an improvisator, and "perhaps, poetry would be no better than what improvisations usually are."

This antipathy to inspiration as a substitute for art may have led to Timrod's writing a defence of the sonnet. It seems more probable that the work was the outgrowth of a heated argument, or of some bit of reading that aroused his mind. Hayne suggests that admiration for Wordsworth was responsible, and that Timrod is defending the form "against the assaults of a large body of depreciators with admirable skill and effect." [24] Whatever the cause, the ideas expressed are Timrod's, and they help to adumbrate his mind.

The essay begins uncompromisingly. There is, first, an aristocratic disdain of popular taste. The sonnet "has never been a popular form of verse;" it is never likely to be. But the popularity and comprehension of a poet's work rarely begin with the multitude. A few cultivated persons understand and explain his work; gradually, after these explanations seep downward, his verses may become popular. In the essay, Timrod makes no attempt to reconcile this doctrine with his belief that the poet must speak what men dimly feel but can not say for themselves.

He is emphasizing the artistry that a completed poem should have. The sonnet is artificial only as all forms of verse are artificial; that it is one of the more difficult forms

[23] Timrod, "The Character and Scope of the Sonnet." For bibliographical details, see note 1 to this essay.

[24] Hayne, *op. cit.*, 26. Hayne gives no hint as to whether these depreciators were personally known to Timrod. In the essay, a scornful reference is made to Samuel Rogers' attack on the sonnet.

means that it presents a greater challenge to the artist. The enforced condensation requires him to order his thought before he writes, to discard the irrelevant and to concentrate on "one leading idea, around which the others are grouped for purposes of illustration only." Since great poetry had been written in the sonnet form, Timrod, a traditionalist, believed that the form was good: the particular result depended upon the individual poet.

In defending the sonnet, Timrod was dealing only with the tangible or objectified form. He was not attempting to define poetry; he was simply arguing the validity of one type. His next essay is an attempt to distinguish between the poem, and poetry. It is a defence of his concept of poetry, written in answer to a direct attack. Both essays are entitled "What is Poetry?" The first is by William J. Grayson; the second is by Timrod.[25]

The disagreement, at least superficially, was one of definition. Grayson was a neo-classicist, Timrod a romantic. Grayson was inclined to answer his question by considering the form; Timrod, by considering the essence or principle of poetry. The argument is in no sense a new one. Aristotle attempted to differentiate between essence and form, at a time when the word *poetry* included practically all imaginative writing; with the de-limitation of the word in English usage, and with no accepted word to signify the older, larger concept, confusion still results. When the scientist Joseph LeConte discussed the nature of poetry, he began by carefully considering the dual nature of the term.

[25] It seems necessary to be specific because at least two of Timrod's biographers have quoted from Grayson's essay and attributed the quotations to Timrod. Since both essays are reprinted in this book, my quotations can easily be restored to their proper context. For the resemblances between Grayson's essay and his unpublished autobiography, see note 1 under Grayson. For bibliographical details, see note 1 to each essay.

The form is verse. In essence, prose addresses only the emotions and the understanding; poetry addresses also the imagination and the aesthetic sense. There can be no clear line of demarcation: although lacking the form, much prose is in essence poetry; and much verse, despite its formal quality, is not poetry.[26]

Grayson allows only the single meaning. Paraphrasing Dr. Johnson, he declares poetry to be "rythmical composition and a poet, one who composes in measure." The peculiar quality of poetry is in the form of arranging words, without regard to the ideas expressed. All other definitions lead to confusion. To him the terms *prose poems* and *poetic prose* seemed "as incongruous as the phrases, round square and oblong circle." Such phrases were simply a "mystical jargon of rapturous superlatives" freely used by the "transcendental oracular school" of Coleridge and his followers. They sought to give to poetry qualities that poetry did not have. An example of this was in Coleridge's defining poetry "as the proper antithesis not of prose but of science. What more is this than to insist on using words contrary to their common acceptation? According to general usage, is not art the proper antithesis of science?" Also, is it not enough to be a good poet, when poetry itself "is the noblest, most refined, pointed and energetic of the two modes by which among all people, thought and emotion are expressed by language"?

By Grayson's standards, all verse is poetry. A casual bit of doggerel belongs to the genre as surely as the finest work of Milton or Shakspere. Once this is allowed, the province of inquiry changes: from asking what it is, we turn to an examination of the quality of a poem. Here, figurative language may be used effectively, but the labelling of a poem

[26] Joseph LeConte, "On the Nature and Uses of Art," in the *Southern Presbyterian Review*, XV: 519-20, Jan., 1863.

as prosy does not mean that the work is prose; it means simply that the writer was a clumsy poet. The intrinsic merit can be judged, but the simple and clear distinction between poetry and prose must remain steadfast.

Grayson's essay infuriated Timrod. He objected particularly to the "illogical confusion of the ideas conveyed by the terms *poem*, and *poetry*," which Grayson had used as identical in reference. A poem is objective, tangible, a thing complete within itself; poetry is subjective, an essence or feeling rather than a definable reality. Then the antithesis to prose becomes, properly, metre; if this is recognized, the question ceases to be how to distinguish poetry from prose, and becomes an inquiry into "those operations of the human faculties, which, when *incarnated* in language, are generally recognized as poetry."

A part of the definition, therefore, turns on the character of the poet. He must have "a more than ordinary sensibility," and out of this characteristic must come a "medium of strong emotion" which can fuse and transform the objects and thoughts which are the material of poetry. From this powerfully emotional imagination there comes naturally a language which differs from the language of prose. The poet's words are sensuous, picturesque, and impassioned; they are short and concrete. Although the thought may be abstract, the poetic expression of that thought must have life, form, and color. Abstract words make the verse prosaic, until the work "no longer calls up the image which it expresses; it merely suggests the thought which it stands for." The poet is not content with words that convey the meaning; he seeks also the most beautiful, in sound and in association, so that his words will "challenge a slight attention to themselves."

The form is important, but it is not all-inclusive. Timrod

is willing to admit that "there may be such a thing as a prose-poem." Yet he admits it reluctantly. Concentrated, heightened thought and emotion find their natural and proper expression in verse. In a long poem, certain parts will inevitably be merely skillful verse, but the artistry of the writer must so fuse these passages with the impassioned poetry that the entire work will be an organic whole.

As criticism, the essay suffers from being a rebuttal as well as an affirmation. The lines of the argument had been drawn in unshaded black and white by another man; they outraged Timrod's sense of the philosophical and the mystical, which he felt to be at the heart of poetry; but the narrow matter-of-factness of the preceding argument made a reasoned answer difficult. He was forced to deny rather than to disprove. The most valuable part of his reply is in the place that he could most tangibly take hold of his adversary's dicta: in the matter of poetic language. Significantly, here, Timrod is on the side of Dante, and not of Wordsworth. He declares that words in themselves have beauty and euphony and concreteness; in this, he answers Grayson convincingly.

In his longest and best essay, "A Theory of Poetry," [27] Timrod develops and completes his earlier attempts at definition. After dismissing briefly Grayson's essay, he considers Poe's dogmatic statements that a long poem is a contradiction in terms and that the poetical sentiment is derived only from the sense of the beautiful.

In response to the first dictum, Timrod presents two answers. One has to do with the reading of poetry. Although a psychal excitement is necessarily transient, it does not follow that poetry must be read in that mood. In fact, the

[27] For bibliographical details, see note 1 to "A Theory of Poetry." See also, on Timrod's idea of a poet's mind, note 108.

reading of the greatest poetry "is characterized . . . by a thoughtful sublimity and the matured and almost inexhaustible strength of a healthy intellect." Granted this quality of mind, the reader need not complete a poem at one sitting to preserve its unity of effect. If he reads the first book of *Paradise Lost*, he will bring to the second and third books all the impressions of his former reading; he will feel a deeper richness as he continues. The mind will be conscious of the vast unity of the poem, so that "its grand purport and harmonious proportions become more and more clearly apparent."

The length of a poem has nothing to do with its excellence. Only the author can know how long a poem should be; and only through "the ordeal of criticism" can the author's success or failure be determined. Timrod admits that he is inclined to consider Dante's *Divine Comedy* as three distinct poems, and Spenser's *Faërie Queene* a succession of poems. The character of the poem and the intention of the poet may be responsible for a lack of unity. But the poet, if he has artistry enough, can impose order and secure unity. Not all of his poem will in the subjective sense be genuine poetry; parts of it will inevitably be verse, but "these parts may be raised so far above the ordinary level of prose by skillful verse as to preserve the general harmony of the poem and materially to insure its unity as a work of art."

With Poe's theory that poetry was limited in subject to "the sense of the beautiful," Timrod dissented vigorously. He was willing to grant the validity of this kind of poetry, and even to admit that Poe had "fixed with some definiteness one phase of its merely subjective manifestation. It is, indeed, to the inspiration which lies in the ethereal, the remote and the unknown, that the world owes some of its sweetest poems; and the poetry of words has never so strange a fascination as when it seems to suggest more than it utters."

But to admit the validity of the kind was not to accept this kind as the only, or even the highest, poetry. Literature is not independent of life, or of truth. The creation of beauty is a sufficient aim for a writer; it is not the highest or noblest aim.

Essentially, Timrod was an ethical critic. He did not propose to limit its scope, but he was convinced that the greatest poetry must have an ethical content. Poe had attempted to reduce the many and varied sources of poetry to a single element, beauty. There are other, equally valid sources: particularly, power and truth. A poem need not be philosophical, but it can embody philosophy; every poet has the right "to make his art the vehicle of great moral and philosophical lessons."

Some miscellaneous ideas garnered from letters, editorials, and poems help to round out Timrod's poetic theory. One concerns standards of poetry. He required a high level of performance of himself; since his mind was not easily malleable, he found it hard to excuse poor work in others. Even brotherly affection could not lead him to pardon bad poetry: "Sissie has been sending me several sheets of her nonsense. Poor girl! She has very little to amuse her, and I found it hard to tell her the truth about them. But of all things in the world, I think a poetaster the most contemptible; and to save myself the discredit of having one for a sister, I have written to her, treating her versicles without mercy." [28] This brutal letter has not survived, and there is no record of his sister's verses.

[28] Letter to Emily, March 25, 1861, in Timrod-Goodwin Collection, South Caroliniana Library. W. P. Trent (*William Gilmore Simms*, 233-34) thinks Timrod's inability to conceal his dislike of poor poetry may have led

Soon after he assumed the editorship of the *Daily South Carolinian,* Timrod wrote an editorial, "To our Poetical Contributors." This was a public performance; also, it may be, Timrod had mellowed somewhat in his opinion of mere versifiers. Whatever the reason, he begins mildly. But the concluding sentences are, under their politeness, as uncompromising as words can well be:

We have a heart to sympathise with all lovers of poetry, not excepting those who are incompetent to appreciate it critically, and who, in consequence, sometimes, mistake its weeds for its flowers. The instinct which leads all men to delight in the musical expression of sentiment is a divine one, and we may not despise it even where its action happens to be vitiated by defects of judgment and taste. Such, indeed, is our reverence for that instinct, that we are inclined to accord some respect even to the writer of bad verse. Indifferent rhyme may occasionally be the offspring of genuine feeling, for poetry is an art in which no one can excel without genius and cultivation. Where, then, the offender has the excuse of natural emotion, we think he ought to be treated with great gentleness. Yet, at the same time, we would advise all in whom the *aura divina* is wanting, to suppress their productions, however unaffected may have been the impulse which led to these compositions. There is no necessity of giving to the public verses, the only merit of which is in the source from which they spring. With regard to the poetical criminal whose inspiration is vanity alone, we have no mercy for him whatever. There ought to be a pillory for the punishment of every evil-doer of this stamp.

We may as well state at the outset, that the standard upon which we have fixed, and by which we shall measure all poetical contributions to our columns, is high, and that to that standard

---

to a temporary estrangement with Simms: "Timrod was critical by nature and Simms was vulnerable in many places. Timrod knew that he could write real poetry, while Simms could not, and it probably vexed him to hear the elder man airing his often crude views upon poetical subjects in his positive Johnsonian manner." For Timrod's attitude toward Simms, see also note 3 to "Literature in the South."

we shall adhere, without reference to any other considerations than those of merit or demerit. While there are in the English language so many exquisite poems not very well known, we shall prefer to give selections from these, or even from authors who, however familiar, can never lose their perennial freshness, than to afflict our critical readers with such effusions as, in the corner of some newspapers, appear under the head of original verse.[29]

One who reads today the poetry that Timrod included may feel that he frequently relaxed his standards. But he was publishing, or quite often reprinting, the work of people whom he knew personally. In addition to his own and some of his father's work, Timrod used many poems by his friends: Hayne, Simms, Bruns, and Requier; several by two men—Harry Lyndon Flash and James Ryder Randall —whom he had met in his days as war correspondent; a poem by Thomas Bailey Aldrich and part of one by Whittier; and quotations from many English poets. He felt himself unduly handicapped: he could not pay for original contributions, and he did not himself receive the papers that came to the office. Even his opportunity to clip and reprint was limited.[30]

A few technical remarks are interesting. In a letter to Hayne, Timrod writes that he has "the right poet's inclination to plunge at once *in medias res.*" [31] In another letter,

[29] Columbia *Daily South Carolinian*, Jan. 19, 1864.
[30] Letter to Hayne, July 10, 1864, in Hubbell, *op. cit.*, 32: "I do not know whether you have published any verses lately, but if so, you may possibly be surprised that they are not copied in the Carolinian. The reason is that I never see a literary paper. Fontaine immediately seizes on them for his wife who keeps them on file. If you should ever wish anything to appear in the Carolinian,—I mean of course after you have sold it to some other paper not too mean to buy it—you must send it to me."
[31] March 30, 1866; quoted in Hubbell, *op. cit.*, 59. On March 7, 1866, Timrod used the same phrase to Hayne, but without relating it to poetry (Hubbell, *op. cit.*, 51): "I like usually to plunge *in medias res.*"

Timrod defends himself against dogmatic remarks by James Wood Davidson; after reading Davidson's criticism of his poetry, Timrod wrote indignantly to Hayne:

Did you mark what the fellow says about the use of *my* & *thy* before vowels? "A well established principle of euphony demands the use of mine & thine. ["] One would think that Mr. Davidson must have scrutinized closely all the great masters, and found this rule invariably observed" [*sic*]. I turn to Tennyson (Talking Oak) and read "And even into *my in*most ring" (D. objects to ["] thy inmost heart"). Again, "Then Close and dark *my arms* I spread"—"Showering thy gleanèd wealth into *my open* breast" &c &c. I could quote a half dozen similar instances. Even this fool's favorite Poe has "My Mother, *my own* Mother who died early." The truth is, of course, that this rule is not, like similar rules in Greek & French, imperative in English. The poet has the privilege of using either form as his ear dictates. Mr Davidson has no ear, and therefore he cannot understand that if I had crunched together so many *ns* as I would have done if I had written "in thine unmingled scorn," so far from consulting the laws of euphony, I should have been guilty of a cacophony. But you know these things as well as I.[32]

To the same friend, he wrote his opinion of prize-poems in general, and specifically of one that Hayne had just published. His criticism is mild, yet exact:

I received your prize poem this morning—thank you for sending it. It is a very noble production indeed—quite worthy of the crown—but may I be so frank as to tell you that its excellence seems to me rather rhetorical than poetical. This fault, however, belongs to all prize-poems,—to mine, I think, in a far greater degree than your own. The poet cannot draw his purest and subtlest strains except from his own unremunerated heart.[33]

[32] To Hayne, March 7, 1866; quoted in Hubbell, *op. cit.*, 52-53.
[33] To Hayne, July 11, 1867; quoted in Hubbell, *op. cit.*, 87-88. Hayne's prize-poem was "The Confederates in the Field;" Timrod's, "Address Delivered at the Opening of the New Theatre at Richmond" (1863).

These are direct statements. Ideas embodied in poems are indirect: they represent the poet speaking dramatically, and not necessarily in his own person. Yet, if evaluated with reasonable caution, the thought in many poems can be read as a valuable extension of his remarks in prose. In varying forms but with the same core of meaning, basic ideas that troubled his mind appear and re-appear.

One is partially objective. The values of the world seemed to him material values; those of poetry were ethical, spiritual, and aesthetic. He could find no way to reconcile these opposites. Yet if poetry were to have meaning for the world, the values of poetry must be accepted by it. Otherwise, a man's poetry became a private possession, and there was little reason for him to put his thought into an objectified form.[34]

Although the period in which he lived was in his estimation less materialistic than the eighteenth century,[35] it felt little need for intellectual and spiritual knowledge. Sometimes the very structure of the world appeared to make this structure of society inevitable: since men were bound to matter, space, and time, then "Communion with the spirit land / Died with the last inventions." It was a prosaic day, in which the world falsified its dreams.[36]

The poem "Youth and Manhood" combines this feeling of the world's indifference with the poet's sense of being aloof, and therefore removed. But he suspects that his youth is a reason for his inhabiting a freer, loftier region: the men

[34] See "A Vision of Poesy" and "A Theory of Poetry"; also, the discussion and notes below; and "A Rhapsody of a Southern Winter Night," in *Poems*, 109-13.

[35] See "A Theory of Poetry."

[36] The poem is titled, perhaps significantly, "A Little Spot of Dingy Earth"; in Cardwell, *Uncollected Poems*, 67-71. The quotations are from pp. 70-71.

who toil and plod may have simply, in the endless strife, lost faith with youth. With a young man's arrogant prayer, Timrod closes his poem:

> If the same toil which indurates the hand
> Must steel the heart,
> Till, in the wonders of the ideal land,
> It have no part;
>
> Oh! take me hence! I would no longer stay
> Beneath the sky;
> Give me to chant one pure and deathless lay,
> And let me die! [37]

The desire for death may have been rhetorical; the feeling which permeates the poem was real. It intensified rather than lessened. When he asked himself, or possibly was asked in such a way that he could not shake the query from his mind, why he did not write more poetry, his feeling about the indifference to that art breaks forth: "the world, in its worldliness, does not miss / What a poet sings." But the writer in objectifying his thought has somehow cast it away from him. Thus the thought, dream, or fancy loses its personal application.[38]

Closely related to this is his feeling that some truths are better left unsaid, that "Too broad a daylight wraps us all." Perhaps Timrod was half-ashamed of the mystical part of his thoughts, and hesitant about voicing them too plainly. He believed that there were impenetrable mysteries, which could be intuitively known and in part understood; he felt that richness was lost when too much was explained. Apparently uncertain in his own beliefs, he knew only that intro-

[37] "Youth and Manhood," in *Poems*, 24-26.
[38] "Why Silent," in *Poems*, 45.

spection lost much when it was forced into the semi-reality of words.[39]

Another phase of his dissatisfaction is most clearly stated in the poem "Retirement." In a dramatic soliloquy, the poet advises a friend that a lonely house awaits them; there the two can build "A wall of quiet thought, and gentle books / Betwixt us and the hard and bitter world." In that retreat, they can shut out unpleasant news, and dally with peaceful thoughts and feelings.[40] Another form of his discontent shows in passages that express an inability to loose his thoughts and at the same time to order and discipline them. The dim monotones of an embryonic poem bewilder his brain "With a specious and cunning appearance of thought / I seem to be catching but never have caught." [41]

He felt, also, that men did not understand or value meditation. If a man worked, even though he labored only at the paltry trade of sonnet-writing, he should have tangible results to show. Men accustomed to a "busy vacancy" had no patience with a man's lying fallow, with simply observing and thinking: he was an idler, and to be sneered at.[42]

These troubled expressions are too much a part of his

[39] Sonnet V, "Some truths there be are better left unsaid"; in *Poems*, 173. The same thought appears also in "A Rhapsody of a Southern Winter Night," 111:

> While in the fears that chasten mortal joy,
> Is one that shuts the lips, lest speech too free,
> With the cold touch of hard reality,
> Should turn its priceless jewels into dust.

He was also convinced that a poet could not fully understand what he intuitively knew or felt. See Sonnet XIV, "Are these wild thoughts, thus fettered in my rhymes," and the poem "Dreams," in *Poems*, 182 and 101-102.

[40] "Retirement," in *Poems*, 136. See also "Sonnet—In the Deep Shadow," in *Uncollected Poems*, 53.

[41] "Vox et Præterea Nihil," in *Poems*, 31.

[42] Sonnet IV, "They dub thee idler, smiling sneeringly," in *Poems*, 172.

mind to be disregarded. His dissatisfaction with his completed work is a compound of many elements.[43] He could occasionally profess an aristocratic disdain of the world's opinion; [44] beyond question, he had a low opinion of mass intelligence. Yet a private art intended for the few seemed to him an imperfect and largely useless art. The poet had a function to perform: to translate for this mass-mind the aspirations and thoughts which, otherwise, it could never grasp.[45] The poet was minister of truth, power, and beauty; he was a responsible agent, performing a function that no other agent could perform.[46]

This may be at the heart of Timrod's discontent. He was confident of his poetic power, yet, judging from his early poems, it seemed to him a power without adequate direction or control. His work was too much abstracted from reality, both within itself and in its audience. It was not enough to write graceful love lyrics or give voice to his personal feelings. In that manner, the poet could find relief

[43] See, for typical examples, "To Anna," in *Uncollected Poems*, 92; "A Vision of Poesy," section II; Sonnet X, in *Poems*, 178; "Why Silent," in *Poems*, 45; also, two letters from Emily Timrod Goodwin to Hayne (Nov. 23, 1867, in Timrod-Goodwin Collection, South Caroliniana Library): "With regard to our brother's age I must be candid with you. The year of his birth was written down by my father as the 8th of December 1829 [actually, W. H. Timrod recorded Henry's birth in his day-book as occurring Dec. 8, 1828]; but Hal always said 1830. He thought he had accomplished so little that he made himself a year younger than he really was." On Oct. 22, 1867, in a letter to Hayne describing his death, Emily wrote (quoted in Hayne, *op. cit.*, 61-62; Ms. in Timrod-Goodwin Collection): "After the Doctor went, he said to me, 'And is this to be the end of all—so soon! and I have achieved so little? I thought to have done so much. I had just before my first attack fallen into a strain of such pure and delicate fancies. I think this winter I would have done more than I have ever done; I should have written more purely, and with greater delicacy.'"

[44] See the opening paragraphs of "The Character and Scope of the Sonnet."

[45] "A Vision of Poesy," in *Poems*, 87-88.

[46] See "A Theory of Poetry;" also note 108.

for his own impatient spirit; but he had not, as artist, attained full manhood.[47]

If this reading of his work is correct, Timrod until 1860 was a poet in search of a theme. Before that time, he found many themes, and he wrote good poems on some of them. But only infrequently did such a poem satisfy him. His concept was noble; in comparison, his performance was inadequate. So he was influenced heavily and directly by the writers he most admired, while he was painfully working out for himself the passage from their ideas to his own.

The war gave him a theme. Timrod was ready for it, with a technique that had become individual to himself, and capable of translating this matter of poetry into poetry itself. Whether rightly or wrongly, he felt that in his theme he had found common ground with his people, that he was giving expression to what they dimly felt. In this poetry the direct and sometimes embarrassing evidences of indebtedness disappear; his thought had grown strong enough to absorb the earlier influences and to transmute them until they become an integral part of his own thought.

The finest and clearest expression of that thought is not in the early (and factually erroneous) paeans to a coming victory.[48] It is rooted in tragedy. In victory as in defeat, the tragedy would remain; and it would be almost equally pitiless for victor and vanquished. Against this tragedy of men Timrod sets the eternal quality of nature with its inherent peacefulness; and he sets against it, also, the faith of human beings. With this sombre awareness of death there came also, in 1865, the personal tragedy of the death of his only son. The man who wrote "Spring," "Christmas," "A Mother's

[47] "A Vision of Poesy," in *Poems*, 88 and 97-99.
[48] The best example of this is the conclusion of "The Cotton Boll," in *Poems*, 11.

Wail," and the final "Ode" had experienced universal emotions.

These poems are not, in the technical sense, major poems, and Timrod is not a major poet. But in them Timrod has magnificently embodied his concept of poetry. When he was simply voicing in restrained and powerful verse the emotions that had become a part of him, he was an authentic poet.

II

A vast amount of Southern intellectual energy was expended, in the years 1830-1860, in presenting arguments and pleas for a regional intellectual independence. These partisan efforts to create a literary nationalism brought little in the way of tangible results. If the discussion was unprofitable, the problem itself was painful, engrossing, and apparently inescapable.[49]

To this forensic arena of bitterness and vexation, Timrod came late.[50] By 1859 the South was almost unified in its opposition to the North. The easy, popular thing to do was to throw hard verbal bricks at Boston and New York. Timrod does his share of this, but he does not absolve his own region of blame or responsibility. The Southern author is "the Pariah of modern literature" because he is caught between hostility and contempt abroad and scornful indifference at home: "It is the settled conviction of the North that genius is indigenous there, and flourishes only in a Northern atmosphere. It is the equally firm conviction of

[49] For an excellent discussion of this subject, see J. B. Hubbell, "Literary Nationalism in the Old South," in *American Studies in Honor of William Kenneth Boyd* (Durham, 1940), pp. 175-220.

[50] With his essay, "Literature in the South" (1859). For bibliographical details, see note 1 to this essay.

the South that genius—literary genius, at least—is an exotic that will not flower on a Southern soil."

Timrod reserves his sharpest thrusts for Southerners. Native writers are neglected because literature is considered an epicurean amusement, and because readers prefer the classical and neo-classical to the modern romantic authors. The writer himself is not esteemed in a land where taste is archaic and judgment is uninformed. Timrod never doubted the superiority of nineteenth-century writing; he was troubled only that readers and teachers seemed frequently to prefer Pope to Wordsworth, and remained oblivious to "that most important revolution in imaginative literature . . . which took place a little more than half a century ago." The men who brought about that revolution had introduced a mystical element into verse, which distinguished it from earlier kinds, and into criticism an analysis which deduced its laws from nature and truth rather than from the authority of particular writers.

Equally provincial and almost equally harmful was the current demand from another group for a superficial "Southernism in literature." It closely resembled the earlier demand for "Americanism in literature," and each meant only that "an author should confine himself in the choice of his subjects to the scenery, the history, and the traditions" of his own section or country. Without any qualification, Timrod labelled this a false and narrow criterion by which to judge of true nationality. It is in the handling of a subject, and not in the subject itself, that the characteristics of a writer are revealed, and "he alone, who, in a style evolved from his own individual genius, speaks the thoughts and feelings of his own deep heart, can be a truly national genius." To such a writer, the circumscription of subjects was foolish and unfortunate. The author must have the right to choose according to his own needs and taste; that he would not thereby lose his nationality was easily proved by the Roman plays of Shakspere and the French novels of Scott.

In January, 1864, Timrod began to write a series of editorials [51] that continue and in part repeat his essay, "Literature in the South." The war, he thinks, has brought about one improvement: the blockade has cut off the supply of English and Northern books, and thus has forced Southerners to read native works. In turn, Southern authors, awake "to the fact that they have at last an audience," have been writing vigorously, and with enough ability to indicate "that a new era of intellectual energy is dawning upon us." These books and the best of the literary magazines and papers show "the national mind struggling to find fit and original expression." If there is much imitation and many indifferent books, there is also evidence that Southern literature is beginning to "trust to its native strength alone." [52]

Although he favored an independence of foreign models and asked for a literature that would reflect and reveal the Southern mind,[53] Timrod did not want a local color literature. He rephrases his earlier concept: "There is but one

[51] On January 13, 1864, the Columbia *Daily South Carolinian* announced in its columns the valedictory of R. W. Gibbes, M. D., and its new ownership by F. G. De Fontaine & Co. De Fontaine was to be editor, and as "associate editor we have secured the services of HENRY TIMROD, ESQ." He was responsible for the editorials; he helped also with other sections of the paper. In a letter to Hayne, Timrod disclaims the authorship of most of the book notices; see page 50 of Introduction. All the editorials that contain literary criticism are printed in the notes to "Literature in the South" and "A Theory of Poetry." J. B. Hubbell, *op. cit.*, 133-45, reprints five of them.

[52] The first of his editorials, entitled "Southern Literature," Jan. 14, 1864.

[53] "Southern Nationality," Jan. 16, 1864, and "Nationality in Literature," Jan. 19, 1864. The quotation in this paragraph is from "Nationality in Literature."

way to be a truly national writer, and that is by being a truly original writer . . . the man of original genius draws his matter from the depth of his own being; and the national character, in which, as a unit of the nation, he shares, finds its utterance through him."

Timrod also considers the parallel demand for a national song. Most songs of this kind he thinks worthless from a literary point of view. "The Star-Spangled Banner" and "Rule Britannia" gained popularity through their effective refrains, and not through any merit as poetry; with the exception of "Maryland, My Maryland," no Southern song attained even that type of popularity. Since people do not choose their songs on the basis of poetic merit, the poets are not to blame. Timrod lists four things as necessary to the success of a national song: "Its verse must run glibly on the tongue; it must contain somewhere, either in a stanza or in a refrain, a sentiment, tersely and musically expressed, which appeals to some favorite pride, prejudice, or passion of the people; it must be married to an effective, but not complicated air, and it must be aided by such a collocation of accidents as may not be computed." The poet even of genius cannot control all of these elements; the Confederacy possessed no writers equal to the task of expressing "the whole great soul of a nation within the compass of a few simple and melodious verses." But the task was worth attempting, and he hoped that writers would, in the effort, "find inspiration enough to draw forth the utmost capacity of their genius." [54]

He was not optimistic. The turbulence and excitement of war might be excellent as a period of germination, but

[54] "National Songs," Jan. 24, 1864. See also his letter to Rachel Lyons, Sept. 6, 1861, in *Southern Literary Messenger*, II: 609, Nov., 1940.

not as a period of growth. Yet the intense emotion which prevents a poet from writing well at the time may give strength and character to his thought. After a period of meditation, which could come only with the return of peace, Southern writers might be able to write great poems.[55]

The editorials themselves suffer from this lack of tranquillity. On August 25, 1864, Timrod described his work to Hayne: "I have not written a line of verse for a twelve-month. All the poetry in my Nature has been fagged out of me I fear. I work very hard,—besides writing the leaders of the paper I often descend into the local column, as you must have noticed by such articles as *Literary Pranks, Arsenal Hill,* and the *Troubles of a Midsummer Night.* My object is to show that a poet can drudge as well [as] a duller man, and therefore I don't complain." [56] It was one thing to drudge uncomplainingly, and presumably Timrod was equal to that task; it was quite another under the circumstances to write with strength and intelligence. Even dwarf essays require a sustained thought that Timrod often seemed unable to give to them.[57]

[55] "War and Literature," Feb. 28, 1864, and an editorial without a title, Sept. 15, 1864.

[56] Quoted in Hubbell, *op. cit.,* 43.

[57] The *Daily South Carolinian* stopped with the burning of Columbia on Feb. 17, 1865. Its printer, Julian A. Selby (*Memorabilia and Anecdotal Reminiscences of Columbia, S. C.,* Columbia, 1905, 101) writes that as Sherman's army approached he and Timrod "issued a 'thumb-sheet' two or three times a day," with shells dropping near the building. Timrod wrote some editorials, 1865-66, for the *Phoenix* (started in Columbia March 21, 1865, but moved before December to Charleston). Trent, *op. cit.,* 292, says that Timrod did not "contribute a line for weeks together." Timrod (letter to Hayne, March 30, 1866; in Hubbell, *op.cit.,* 60) writes that Fontaine "started the Carolinian" again in Charleston: "I have hacked for him for four months, and have not yet received one month's pay. The truth is, Fontaine *can't* pay."

III

Few writers have ever indicated so precisely the major influences upon their art as Timrod did. He expressed frequently and quite frankly his indebtedness to Wordsworth; he praised the work of Milton and of Tennyson; and he is said to have completed a metrical translation of the poems of Catullus.[58] Although he knew the works of many other poets, these four influenced him most directly and immediately. Hayne notes that "his reading was more exact than varied. His unerring critical tact rejected the false and meretricious; but for authors of his deliberate choice, his affection daily increased." [59]

First in his affection was Wordsworth. In the morning of his career, writes his close friend Hayne, "Timrod looked up to Wordsworth as his poetical guide and exemplar." [60] Wordsworth seemed not only his personal mentor, but the guiding spirit of poetry in his time: "The poet who first taught the few simple but grand and impressive truths which have blossomed into the poetic harvest of the nineteenth century was Wordsworth . . . When he began to write, it was with the purpose of embodying in all the poetic forms at his command the two truths of which the poets and readers of his time seemed to him completely incognizant. These were, first, that the materials and stimulants of poetry might be found in the commonest things about us; and second, behind the sights, sounds, and hues of external nature there is 'something more than meets the senses, something undefined and unutterable which must

---

[58] J. P. K. Bryan, in Introduction, *Poems,* xxxiii.
[59] Hayne, *op. cit.,* 18-19.
[60] *Ibid.,* 21.

be felt and perceived by the soul' in its moments of rapt contemplation. This latter feeling it is that constitutes the chief originality of Wordsworth." In Timrod's estimation, this feeling did not appear in Shakspere or his contemporaries, in Milton or his followers, in Dryden, Pope, Thomson, or Cowper. But it "has been caught up and shadowed forth" by every poet from Byron to Tennyson.[61]

An individual adumbration of this feeling or idea appears in Timrod's poetry. He felt himself to be in the tradition of Wordsworth.[62] When a correspondent suggested to him that his poem "Katie" was Byronic in tone, Timrod answered that the resemblance was "merely a *verbal* one," and that the particular couplet under discussion is "made the text of a train of sentiment which is much more *Wordsworthian* than Byronic in its character." [63]

This admitted influence permeates his work in the decade 1850-60. The need for dealing with common and hu-

[61] "A Theory of Poetry."

[62] In a thoughtful discussion of Timrod's life and work, Peirce Bruns (in *Conservative Review*, I: 268, May, 1899) disagreed flatly with this; but he apparently was not familiar with Timrod's prose: "It has been said that he was most deeply influenced by Wordsworth. But this is manifestly erroneous. The mistake, we suppose, has arisen from Paul Hayne's statement that Timrod's favorite poem was Wordsworth's 'Intimations of Immortality from Recollections of Early Childhood,' a poem which is certainly the most un-Wordsworthian of all the Lake Poet's works. Surely there can be no resemblance between the 'cloudy pantheism' of Wordsworth and the clear-cut, definite forms under which Timrod envisaged the flowers of nature. Timrod, in this regard, at least, is far nearer to Shelley."

Trent, *op.cit.*, 235, states without qualification of Timrod: "That he was dominated by Tennyson . . . is perfectly true."

There are obvious borrowings in thought from Wordsworth's "Ode on Intimations of Immortality" in Timrod's "Dramatic Fragment," *Poems*, 105-06.

[63] Letter to Rachel Lyons, in "Unpublished Letters of Henry Timrod," edited by William Fidler, *Southern Literary Messenger*, II: 610-11, Nov., 1940.

man things is emphasized by the angel of Poesy in the
"Vision;" [64] it is explicitly stated by Timrod in a sonnet on
poetry:

> POET! if on a lasting fame be bent
> Thy unperturbing hopes, thou will not roam
> Too far from thine own happy heart and home;
> Cling to the lowly earth, and be content!
> So shall thy name be dear to many a heart;
> So shall the noblest truths by thee be taught;
> The flower and fruit of wholesome human thought
> Bless the sweet labors of thy gentle art.
> The brightest stars are nearest to the earth,
> And we may track the mighty sun above,
> Even by the shadow of a slender flower.
> Always, O bard, humility is power!
> And thou mayst draw from matters of the hearth
> Truths wide as nations, and as deep as love.[65]

This was not a plea for a limited provincialism. Rather,
it represents his belief that universality could be secured
through the method of handling immediate and well-
known objects, and through giving a new richness to ordinary things.

The major influence of Wordsworth is to be found in
Timrod's concept of nature. Although he knew the classical
poets and drew intellectual sustenance from them, he spoke
truly of having "fed my muse with English song / Until her
feeble wing grew strong." [66] In particular it had fed upon
the intuitive, contemplative mysticism of the romantic
poets. That his own concept of nature deviated from
Wordsworth's somewhat, he consciously realized; but he

---

[64] "A Vision of Poesy," in *Poems*, 86-89 and 99.
[65] *Poems*, 169.
[66] "A Dedication," in *Poems*, 37.

knew likewise that he had started from Wordsworth's premise.

Both men are conscious of spiritual qualities no longer understood; instead of setting this consciousness in the period before birth and in early childhood, Timrod feels that he must some time, some where, have existed in a finer and more sensitive form:

> O mother! somewhere on this lovely earth
> I lived, and understood that mystic tongue,
> But, for some reason, to my second birth
> Only the dullest memories have clung.[67]

For both poets, these memories can best be stimulated by nature.

In Timrod's view, nature can provide an ethical basis for poetry; she is so bountiful that her lessons "may be gathered from the very dust we tread beneath our feet." [68] He admits that it is possible to disregard truth and yet to write good poetry, by concentrating on subjective beauty. Even in attaining this narrow end, nature can help the writer. Timrod grants readily that there need be no moral shut within the bosom of the rose; equally, that poems may be judged, without regard to morality, in "simple reference to their poetical effect." The contemplative or philosophical poet is "influenced by a vaster purpose . . . [he] aims to create beauty also, but . . . desires at the same time to mould this beauty into the shape of a temple dedicated to Truth." Beauty is implicit, but is made to serve a loftier end: in Milton, to justify God's ways to man; in Words-

[67] "A Vision of Poesy," in *Poems*, 78. In the poem "Dramatic Fragment," 105-06, he says that "We are born . . . in miniature completeness;" we do not change, but only grow and develop; and childhood is "a sort of golden daylight."

[68] "A Theory of Poetry." Later quotations in this paragraph are from the same essay.

worth, to give meaning to natural phenomena and richness to familiar things.

Timrod tried to accept Wordsworth's view of a beneficent, all-healing, wisdom-bestowing nature. It represented to him a tenable ideal and a way to contentment. But his own unquiet spirit and his first-hand observation frequently contradicted the words of the older poet. He recommended a study of Wordsworth to Rachel Lyons, in significant words: "I am quite sure that nobody could devote a month or many months to that grand old bard, without being made wiser and better. I myself would be a far happier man if I could follow his teaching, rather than my own dark and perturbed spirit." [69] This happiness he could never attain.

In "The Summer Bower," Timrod describes a secret covert, deep in the woods, that he had often gone to when depressed by grief or distressed by joy. There, usually, he "found the calm I looked for, or returned/Strong with the quiet rapture in my soul." One day, "most sick in mind," he sought this tranquil place, but he found there no comfort for vain repinings, sickly sentiments, or inconclusive sor-

---

[69] Fidler, *op. cit.*, II: 651. Emily Timrod Goodwin, in writing of her brother's love of nature, did not mention the influence of Wordsworth, but emphasized the influence of their mother (Letter, Emily to Hayne, Sept. 25, 1872, in Timrod-Goodwin Collection, South Caroliniana Library; quoted in Hayne, p. 41): "It was from *her,* more than from his gifted father, that my brother derived that intense, passionate love of Nature which so distinguished him. Its sights and sounds always afforded her extreme delight. Shall I ever forget the almost childish rapture she testified, when, after a residence in the pent-up city all her life, she removed with me to the country? A walk in the woods to her was food and drink, and the sight of a green field was joy inexpressible.

"From my earliest childhood, I can remember her love for flowers and trees and for the stars; how she would call our attention to the glintings of the sunshine through the leaves; to the afternoon's lights and shadows, as they slept quietly, side by side; and even to a streak of moonlight on the floor."

rows. Nature had sympathy and medicinal virtue for human suffering, but only "In her own way and with a just reserve;" for a certain kind of introspective suffering—a kind that Timrod knew only too well—nature had no balm:

> But for the pains, the fever, and the fret
> Engendered of a weak, unquiet heart,
> She hath no solace; and who seeks her when
> These be the troubles over which he moans,
> Reads in her unreplying lineaments
> Rebukes, that, to the guilty consciousness,
> Strike like contempt.[70]

The fault was in himself, he thought, and not in nature.

As poet Timrod was scrupulously honest with himself. He could not use material that had not become a part of his being, no matter what powerful sanction that material might have. What he could do was convict himself of lacking philosophy and understanding. In an article written immediately after Timrod's death, William Gilmore Simms traces this lack of certainty to a lack of profundity: "he labored in no field of metaphysics; he simply sang . . . with a native gift, of the things, the beauties, and the charms of nature. He belonged, in the classification of literary men, to the order that we call the contemplative; and without the deeper studies and aims of Wordsworth, he yet belonged to his school . . . The fields, the wayside, the evening twilight, stars and moon, and faint warblings of the birds in green thickets—these were the attractions for his muse. These he meditated in song and sonnet, and his songs emulated all the gentle intuition of nature." [71]

Simms had only a partial understanding of Timrod. The

---

[70] "The Summer Bower," in *Poems*, 106-08.

[71] W. G. Simms, "The Late Henry Timrod," in *Southern Society*, I: 18-19, Oct. 12, 1867; also in Hubbell, *op. cit.*, 153-65.

qualities he describes are profusely scattered through the poems: Timrod was observant, with a quick eye and retentive mind; he wrote many descriptive passages that are accurate and beautiful. The external properties of nature provided a suitable poetic framework. In his best work, the function of nature was more fundamental, more integral, than decoration or the kind of intuition that Simms described. Nature typified the best aspects of life; it hinted at things about which man could only guess. When war came, this peaceful, eternal force contrasted with man's inhumanity and shortsightedness.

Although less pervasive, the influence of Tennyson was equally direct. Timrod's friends in Charleston first detected that influence in his poem "The Arctic Voyager;" [72] since Timrod borrowed obviously and freely from Tennyson's "Ulysses" in thought and in structure, detection was easy and inevitable. Even more directly derived from "Ulysses" is the beginning of "Lines to R. L.": "That which we are and shall be is made up / Of what we have been." [73] Timrod develops this idea through the entire poem, in a manner individual enough; he is writing to a young lady, and his mood is removed from that of "Ulysses." Perhaps he wished deliberately to call Tennyson's poem to the reader's mind, for contrast. The borrowing is too plain not to be intentional.

Timrod liked the dramatic soliloquy. He used the form

[72] Hayne, *op. cit.*, 24.

[73] "Lines to R. L.", in *Poems*, 131. An allusion which takes for granted a knowledge of Tennyson is given in "Lines," *Poems*, 191:

> I saw, or dreamed I saw, her sitting lone,
> Her neck bent like a swan's, her brown eyes thrown
> On some sweet poem—his, I think, who sings
> Œnone, or the hapless Maud:

"Lines" was first published in *Russell's Magazine*, VI: 459, Feb. 1860.

effectively in such poems as "A Dramatic Fragment," "The Summer Bower," and "A Rhapsody of a Southern Winter Night." From Tennyson, also, Timrod adapted the form of "Break, Break, Break" for his own poem, "Hark to the Shouting Wind," although he makes subtle and interesting changes both in the metrics and the idea.

This general indebtedness to Tennyson, likewise, was openly stated in "A Theory of Poetry;" in fact, Timrod implies that he was aware of it earlier than Hayne was. In treating Poe's theory of poetry, Timrod notes that it leads inevitably to the conclusion that Tennyson is the noblest poet who ever lived, and also to the conclusion that Poe is second only to Tennyson. After acquitting Poe of any petty vanity, Timrod adds: "I yield to few, and only to that extravagant few who would put him over the head of Milton himself, in my admiration of Poe, and I yield to none in a love which is almost a worship of Tennyson, with whose poems I have been familiar from boyhood, and whom I yet continue to study with ceaseless profit and pleasure. But I can by no means consent to regard him as the first of Poets." Tennyson's accomplishment is broader and finer than Poe's theory would provide for: his "large nature touches Poe on the one side and Wordsworth on the other."

His most striking comment on Tennyson reveals that Timrod was conscious of a softness and immaturity in some poems. He had met a young lady who seemed passionately fond of poetry, but who had "not yet got beyond the period which goes into ecstasies over Locksley Hall, and into sleep over *In Memoriam*." [74]

[74] Typed copy of letter to Emily, from Charleston, Feb. 10, 1862, in Timrod-Goodwin Collection, South Caroliniana Library. The original is missing.

Timrod's copy of Tennyson has survived, but there is little to be learned from a study of his light markings. The pocket-size volume, now re-bound, is badly worn and the opening pages have been lost; on the fly-leaf, Timrod's wife has written: "This volume of Tennyson belonged to Henry Timrod. He carried it constantly, for many, many years." [75] But any significant notes were made elsewhere: with the exception of his Catullus, Timrod did not annotate his books.

That he considered Milton superior to Tennyson and possibly even to Wordsworth is made clear in "A Theory of Poetry." Timrod's analysis of *Paradise Lost* is based on close study of the poem. But it is difficult to find in his work such unmistakable echoes as can be found of Wordsworth and Tennyson. Technically, he took from Milton the extended simile, and it retained its place after the influence of Tennyson had been so completely absorbed that it disappears. In "The Cotton Bill," the lines beginning "As men who labor in that mine / Of Cornwall" indicate how completely he had made this poetic device his own.[76]

[75] While she owned the book, Mrs. Lloyd wrote to W. A. Courtenay (March 15, 1898; letter in *Memories of the Timrod Revival 1898-1901*, Charleston Library Society): "I have a little worn copy of Tennyson which he always carried with him. It never left him. He had it from the time when he was almost a boy. It is marked by him, and some of the pages turned down by him." It may be noted that Mrs. Lloyd was frequently given to over-statement.

The one pencilled note deals with the line from Section II of "The Princess": "The Rhodope that built the pyramid." Timrod noted: "Herodotus says that this pyramid wrongly ascribed by some to Rhodope was built by Mycerinus." This testifies more to a knowledge of the Greek historian ("Euterpe," Ch. CXXXIV) than to his known appreciation of Tennyson. Timrod has also marked a few lines in "Œnone," in "The Palace of Art," in "A Dream of Fair Women," in "In Memoriam," and in "Maud."

[76] For another example, see *Poems*, 136-37. Timrod's eight volume set of Milton (London: Pickering, 1851) is now in the Timrod Museum at Florence, S. C. It reveals no notes or markings; presumably Timrod owned

The influence of Browning is slight, and readily apparent in only one poem, "Præceptor Amat." Here the resemblance is one of form rather than of thought: Timrod employs the couplet in a manner similar to that of "My Last Duchess," and the poem is a dramatic monologue rather than a soliloquy. But Timrod's whimsical story of the emotions of a tutor seems frequently to embody the mannerisms and verbal obscurities of Browning for the effect of parody. It seems evident, from his remarks in "A Theory of Poetry," that Timrod considered himself well-acquainted with the works of Robert and Elizabeth Barrett Browning, but that his admiration had been partly checked by some over-enthusiastic admirers. A theory of poetry could be drawn from their practice, he notes; but it would exclude many other excellent poets. The application of this doctrine was the work of their followers. In 1866 he complains of Davidson's "*niaiseries* in regard to Wordsworth and Mrs Browning." [77]

The influence of Shelley has been previously treated. That of Keats appears to be negligible, although certain

---

a copy of Milton earlier. On a fly-leaf, in Timrod's writing but without a date, is the notation, "from his esteemed, departed friend, Mrs. Emma P. Blake." The material in the Timrod Museum has only association or sentimental value.

[77] Letter to Hayne, March 7, 1866; in Hubbell, *op. cit.*, 54. In an undated letter to Emily from Copse Hill (probably May or August, 1867; Timrod-Goodwin Collection, South Caroliniana Library) he described Jean Ingelow as a "worthy successor of Mrs. Browning's"; and on Aug. 24, 1864, he closed an editorial on the imperfections of contemporaneous judgments with her "titanic lines," beginning "Every age, / Through being beheld too close, is ill-discerned / By those who have not lived past it." Ludwig Lewisohn (*Books We Have Made*, 53; scrapbook in Charleston Library Society, from Charleston *News and Courier*, Sundays July 5-Sept. 20, 1903) suggests that "A 'Dramatic Fragment' is an attempt in the jerky, but picturesque, blank verse of Elizabeth Barrett Browning."

personal similarities in the lives of the two men have called forth unconvincing comparisons of their work.[78]

The poems in Timrod's *Autographic Relics*,[79] mainly written in the 1840's, reveal a marked indebtedness to the lyrics of Byron [80] and the lyrics and anacreontics of Moore. This was a transitory influence, but in Timrod's youth it was a strong one. Although he published in 1857 a poem strongly reminiscent of Moore, he indicated in the same magazine a realization of Moore's superficiality.[81]

Timrod's early liking for James Thomson lasted longer than his fondness for Moore. One of his earliest poems (dated 1843), has beside it a note, "Written in a blank leaf of Thompson's Castle of Indolence;" the nine-line poem makes a comparison between the English poet's dream country, where he "created a fancied realm," and the "sad

[78] See page 5 of introduction, and "A Vision of Poesy," in *Poems*, 90. The semi-personal, semi-literary comparison is well illustrated by L. Frank Tooker's comment (in the *Century*, LV, n.s. 33: 932-34, April, 1898): "The reader is constantly reminded of the cumulative sadness that was the lot of Keats, as he is reminded of the latter's excessive sensibility of temperament. Indeed, in spirit the two poets were essentially kin, though in poetic insight and expression—in the true province of the poet—Timrod, of course, dwelt on a lower plane. He also dwelt in a different atmosphere, for while the influence of Keats may be traced in his work, the feeling, the local coloring, the habit of thought, are his own."

[79] Ms. in Charleston Library Society. These poems have all been published in Cardwell, *The Uncollected Poems of Henry Timrod* (1942).

[80] Hayne, who disliked Byron, expressly notes (p. 67) "the absence from his works of all morbid arraignments of the Eternal justice or mercy; all blasphemous hardihood and whining complaint—in a word, all *Byronism* of sentiment."

[81] "Song—When I bade thee adieu," published in *Russell's Magazine*, I: 489, Sept. 1857; in *Uncollected Poems*, 108; the opening section of "The Character and Scope of the Sonnet," (*Russell's*, May, 1857) reveals his doubt of Moore's validity as a poet. The manuscript poem is in *Autographic Relics*, and may have been written several years earlier. I fully agree with Cardwell (*op. cit.*, 3-4) that "in spirit and subject matter, Timrod's early verse seems much like the poetry of Moore."

reality" of a Carolina school room.[82] Thomson's handling
of nature seemed too matter-of-fact for Timrod to rate him
as a truly significant poet: he had concentrated too much
on description, and neglected the symbolic meaning.[83]

Timrod's knowledge of Chaucer may have been slight.
Once, in celebrating the flower that he loved so well, Tim-
rod mentions that a daisy called to mind that these were
"Chaucer's favorites, little pink-tipped stars." [84]

Timrod's highest tribute to Spenser was embodied in an
editorial attacking England for her pretended neutrality:
"there are few of us so free from the strong spell of her great
literature as to be able to hate her without considerable
reluctance." In contrast to England's materialism, one remembers "the ethereal enchantments of SPENSER, and in
recalling that he too, that mystic wanderer into fairyland,
was one of her children, we are well nigh seduced into be-
lieving that a land which has given birth to so divine a
creature cannot be organically affected by a vice so inconsistent with the character of its offspring." [85] This admiration for Spenser's work may indicate that the Elizabethan
poet had not become a favorite until late in life. Hayne sug-

[82] "In Bowers of Ease," in *Autographic Relics*, and in *Uncollected Poems*,
78; see also 119, n. 68. Timrod consistently spells the poet's name Thompson; a few editions show this spelling, and Timrod may have owned one
of them.
Worth noting among these very early poems is Timrod's parody of
Charles Wolfe's "The Burial of Sir John Moore after Corunna." The first
two lines show its schoolboy, mock-occasional character: "Not a grin was
seen, not a giggle heard / As the tutor breath'd his last." The poem is described as "his first known effort," but is dated 1844. It is printed in
Uncollected Poems, 23.
[83] See "A Theory of Poetry."
[84] "Field Flowers," in *Uncollected Poems*, 100.
[85] Editorial without title, *Daily South Carolinian*, Aug. 3, 1864. The only
other author named is Shakspere; Timrod contrasts England's narrowness
of policy with his universal sympathies. The newspaper's spelling: etherial.

gests, however, that the metrical form of "A Vision of Poesy" is "that employed by Shakspeare in his 'Venus and Adonis,' by Spenser in his 'Astrophel,' and Cowley in his least ambiguous verses." [86]

The songs of Burns Timrod praises mildly; he notes that they have become a folk possession—possibly after they had been talked about and drawn to general attention by a few discerning men.[87] In an editorial on the appropriateness of the names of the months, he calls the Scottish poet as witness: "We have Burns' authority for asserting that 'November chill blows loud with angry sough.'" [88] Timrod's work belongs in a later tradition, and Burns influenced him only as his songs had become a part of a larger current of thought.

Timrod used Shakspere's works freely and with evident familiarity. But this use is primarily as a source of allusions that would not require explanation. When he was competing in a contest that seemed to require references to dramatic characters, he employed brief descriptions and personifications of Lear, Hamlet, Juliet, and Miranda; [89] when he sought a fit and concluding epithet to express his sense of indebtedness to England, he wrote "Shakespeare's

[86] Hayne, op. cit., 31; see also "A Theory of Poetry."

[87] See "The Character and Scope of the Sonnet."

[88] "Names of Months Phonetically Expressive," in Hayne, op. cit., 50-51. Hayne gives no source, but says that it was written "after the surrender at Appomattox." Somewhat similar remarks appear in the Daily South Carolinian, Oct. 2 and 4, 1864, but there Timrod says: "The reader must, himself, make what he can of November. We don't like the month, and shall, therefore, say nothing about it."

[89] "Address Delivered at the Opening of the New Theatre at Richmond," in Poems, 69-73. See also "Field Flowers," in Uncollected Poems, 99-102; and the later, revised version, "Two Field Flowers," in Hubbell, op. cit., 128-30.

England." [90] His liking for Shakspere may have been inherited. His father had, in his boyhood, read the plays by moonlight, and had considered Shakspere "his favorite companion." [91]

Shakspere was used, once, as justification. In a letter to Hayne, Timrod objects bitterly to Simms' describing him as indolent and on one occasion reading a "yellow-covered novel. Now I remember the occasion very well. I was really sick with a most painful malady—a *stricture*, but I didn't tell him that—and I was reading Shakspeare. I have not read ten novels in as many years, and I never read trash, not even Mr. Simms." [92]

When Timrod was dying, two lines from Shakspere troubled him with their haunting precision. He wondered at first if he could not will himself to live;[93] but the next day he quoted Milton's "Death reigns triumphant," and, after that, he "asked me if I remembered the lines from Shakespeare's King John, he had quoted to me on our last walk on the meadow back of Mrs. Stack's house. These lines commence—

> And none of you will bid the winter come
> And thrust his icy fingers in my maw,

etc and alludes to the fearful consuming internal fires from which the dying Monarch suffered. He said I little thought I should suffer from what in reading those lines had caused

[90] "A Dedication," in *Poems*, 38.

[91] Letter from Emily Timrod Goodwin to Hayne, quoted in Hayne, *op. cit.*, 9, and in Hubbell, *op. cit.*, 170. The romantic story may not, however, have impressed Henry as much as it did Emily.

[92] June 4, 1867; quoted in Hubbell, *op. cit.*, 83.

[93] Letter, Emily Timrod Goodwin to Hayne, Oct. 22, 1867 (in Timrod-Goodwin Collection, South Caroliniana Library). Timrod thought that he might "make an effort, like Mrs. Dombey," and regain his health.

me so much horror." [94] This is graphic testimony to the power that Shakspere's lines could wield on his thought.

That he knew something of Shakspere's contemporaries Timrod reveals in the course of a letter to Hayne, lambasting "this 'milk & water' Dennis of Southern criticism," James Wood Davidson. Dekker's lines "about Christ's being 'the first true gentleman that ever breathed,' had never fallen on Mr Davidson's ear. By-the-way, Mr Simms has in more than one place attributed that passage to Middleton. I have assured him over and over again that he was mistaken, but to no purpose. Please show him, when you next meet, the passage in the last scene of the 1st Part of 'The Honest Whore.'" [95]

Although he wrote many love lyrics, he does not seem to have been drawn into the cavalier or metaphysical tradition. One sonnet has the old and well-worn poetic idea that Marvell expresses magnificently in "To His Coy Mistress;" a few lines, especially, remind one of that earlier poem:

> So everywhere on earth,
> This foothold where we stand with slipping feet,
> The unsubstantial and substantial meet,
> And we are fooled until made wise by time.[96]

But the metaphysical style was not intellectually in fashion. Timrod's poetry seems nearer to it than does the poetry of most of his contemporaries. Hayne, who disliked such in-

---

[94] Letter from Emily Timrod Goodwin to Edith Goodwin, Oct. 29, 1867, in Timrod-Goodwin Collection, South Caroliniana Library. A letter from Emily Goodwin to Hayne (Oct. 22, 1867; see note 93) describes the same incident in a slightly different form.

[95] Letter to Hayne, March 7, 1866, Hubbell, *op. cit.*, 54. Hubbell identifies the Simms attribution as in *Beauchampe* (New York, 1856), p. 118. Timrod mentions this erroneous identification again in a letter to Hayne, March 26, 1867 (Hubbell, *op. cit.*, 76). Hayne, *op. cit.*, 56, also talks of Timrod's quoting Ford or Fletcher.

[96] Sonnet XI, in *Poems*, 179.

tellectual daring, writes that "A Cry to Arms" contains "one of the few palpable conceits I can recall, which would seem not merely admissible, but charming." [97]

Timrod seems equally removed from the cavalier tradition. He makes only a casual reference to Suckling; otherwise, his knowledge of these poets must be by assumption only, and any indebtedness must be proved by rather doubtful parallels.[98]

That he was fundamentally religious is made clear in many poems and letters. His fondness for the Hebrew stories and characters in the Bible led naturally in his poetry to references and allusions; two poems, in fact, depend largely upon such extended reference for body and meaning.[99] These poems reveal only a knowledge and use of easily available, well-known material. It may be, subjectively, that Timrod made a close association between the Bible and poetry, but hesitated to put this idea into writing. In a paragraph which he wrote and then deleted, Timrod identifies the spirit of poetry as second only to that of re-

[97] *Poems*, 144-46. Hayne, *op. cit.*, 37, gives it as "A Call to Arms." Two of the mild conceits from the poem, and typical of the kind that Timrod wrote, are:

> And feed your country's sacred dust
> With floods of crimson rain!
>
> .   .   .   .   .
> Does any falter? let him turn
>   To some brave maiden's eyes,
> And catch the holy fires that burn
>   In those sublunar skies.

I suspect that Hayne was referring to the second example, or possibly to the personification of the Southern woman as the lily, and the man as the palm-tree.

[98] Letter to Rachel Lyons, Feb. 3, 1862, in *Southern Literary Messenger*, II: 646, Dec., 1940. See also note 114.

[99] "Madeline" was first published in *The Southern Literary Messenger*, XVIII: 212, April, 1852; in *Poems*, 32-36. "La Belle Juive," in the *Charleston Daily Courier*, Jan. 23, 1862; in *Poems*, 57-59; Timrod enclosed a manuscript copy to Rachel Lyons in his letter to her, Jan. 20, 1862.

ligion: "The sentiment of poetry as it thus developed in the mind is the very ground on which (apart from Revelation) we base our hopes of immortality & this fact should make it the next sacred thing to the great chart of Salvation." [100] Although he discarded the statement as part of his address, Timrod undoubtedly believed it to be truth.

Any reconstruction of Timrod's reading must necessarily be incomplete. As a rule, his references are casual and suggestive, but the samplings indicate a rather exact knowledge of English poetry, and a wider acquaintance than Hayne implies. Some of his estimates of authors and side remarks have a penetrating incisiveness, though they are incomplete and at best give only a partial picture.

In his essays, Timrod quotes from many sources. In addition to those already noted, he lifted illustrative bits from such writers as Francis Bacon,[101] Charles Lamb, Matthew Arnold, Arthur Henry Hallam, John Sterling, Henry Taylor, and Aubrey de Vere. He expressed great admiration for Coleridge, whom he called the noblest critic that ever lived, and he quoted or paraphrased both from the prose and the poetry. Since Timrod's own work was frequently appearing in them, he must have been familiar with the diverse material in the *Southern Literary Messenger* and *Russell's Magazine*. It seems probable that he was also well acquainted with the easily available English and Northern magazines.[102] His quotations and remarks display only that knowledge for which he had an immediate use.

[100] See note 13 to "A Theory of Poetry."

[101] His three-volume set of Bacon (*Novum Organum, Advancement of Learning,* and *Essays*) is in the Timrod Museum at Florence, S. C. It is not marked or annotated.

[102] Both *Russell's* and the *Messenger* used many brief quotations from English authors and magazines. Timrod himself, or a colleague, inserted many short pieces into the columns of the *Daily South Carolinian* in 1864: items from or about Carlyle, Thackeray, Dickens, Wilkie Collins, Lamb,

Thus, a hasty answer to a sister's question gives his opinion of the work of Charlotte Brontë: "I have not time to
write a criticism of Villette; but I agree with most people
that it is inferiour to Jane Eyre. It is by no means a bread
and butter thing however." He comments briefly on the
naturalness of the characters, but thinks the "conclusion
of the book is a specimen of claptrap unworthy of the author
of Jane Eyre. . . . You have heard me admire Miss
Bronte's skill in sky- and weather-painting. There are many
such pictures in this book; but their style is more ambi-
tious than those in Jane Eyre and Shirley—they are less
simple, sketchy, and graphic, and I don't like them half so
well. However, the moonlight scene in the park is magnificent." [103] Timrod's opinion of Charlotte's sisters remains
unknown.

Hayne's belief that Timrod read with more exactness
than variety is partially borne out by Timrod's frank statement that an outside stimulus was responsible for his reading Ovid and Persius.[104] Yet in the war and post-war years

Sidney Smith, Herbert, Cotton, Lamartine, Artemus Ward, Josh Billings,
Whittier, T. B. Aldrich, and so on. The editorial shears apparently worked
on English, Northern, and Southern papers without much discrimination;
probably, on whatever came to hand. In writing to the South Carolina
author Clara Dargan, asking her for contributions to a proposed paper,
Timrod said that her story, "Philip, My Son," "in my opinion, would compare favourably with the best of Blackwood's" (quoted in Hubbell, *op. cit.*,
90). On May 5, 1864, he editorialized hotly about an "extract from an
article" by Oliver Wendell Holmes in the *Atlantic Monthly.* Holmes is
called an "objurgatory doctor," though perhaps an honest abolitionist; but
in response to Holmes' question as to what stand Tennyson and Dickens
have taken on slavery, Timrod answers that Dickens "has probably pene-
trated the true character of the political PECKSNIFFS of the North," and
that Tennyson's "pure and lofty name" has been taken in vain by "the small
Boston versifier."

[103] Letter from Henry to Emily, July 29, 1853, in Timrod-Goodwin Collection, South Caroliniana Library.

[104] Letters to Hayne, March 7, 1866 and March 26, 1867; quoted in
Hubbell, *op. cit.*, 54 and 76.

there is another side to the picture. Books were scarce, and difficult to obtain. In December of 1861 he wrote that the "camp is *life*," and that there were "No new books, no reviews, no appetizing critiques, no literary correspondence, no intellectual intelligence of any kind!" [105] He continued to feel a need for books and magazines, but mainly he did without them. Even his position as an editor did not help much, as he explained to Hayne: "You are aware that it is the rule of all papers and periodicals that the books which are sent to be noticed are the perquisites of him who criticizes them. Having 'noticed' one or two books, and finding that Fontaine took possession of them notwithstanding, I reminded him of the rule, when he said that for the future then, he would notice the books himself. One pleasant consequence of this is that his wretched criticisms are credited to me by the public, while all my leaders are attributed to him." [106]

This desire for new books became more acute. Timrod felt himself out of the current of intellectual thought; he expressed this discontent to his more fortunate friend, and incidentally gives an excellent criticism of Augusta Evans Wilson:

> I have read (skippingly) St Elmo. Somebody lent it to my wife—I could not have got it otherwise—for nobody sends me books or magazines, and of course I can't purchase them. I have yet to see Jane [*sic*] Ingelow, Swinburne,[107] and Robert Buchanan—each of whom I long to be acquainted with. Nor have

[105] Letter to Rachel Lyons, Dec. 10, 1861 (in University of Alabama Library).

[106] Letter to Hayne, July 10, 1864; quoted in Hubbell, *op. cit.*, 32.

[107] By July 11, 1867, Timrod was familiar enough with Swinburne's work to write Hayne (Hubbell, *op. cit.*, 88): "Your criticism of Swinburne also pleases me much; but I must express my regret that you have left his obscurity untouched."

I read a line of Simm's [sic] Serial—nor laid my eyes upon a single number of the "Old Guard."

I quite agree with you with regard to St Elmo, and the character of Miss Evan's [sic] talents. I met her, you know, in Mobile—took tea with her several evenings in succession. She talks well, but pedantically now and then; though not so pedantically as she writes. She has very peculiar, but very false and shallow opinions about poetry and poets.[108]

Later in the month, Timrod again wrote to Hayne, expressing eagerness over a possible visit to Copse Hill. In addition to the "aromatic pine-land atmosphere" and the "happy prospect of your own society," Timrod adds that he is also tempted because "you speak of the publishers sending you their *new books!* You can afford to put up with what Mr. Simms really appears to consider appetizing fare, so unctuously does he refer to it (I mean 'hog and hominy') if, mean time, instead of having your imagination starved, it (or she?) is free to wander in fresh literary pastures." [109]

In less than a week, according to Hayne, Timrod was at Copse Hill, for a "month's sojourn." The two men sauntered through the pine forest, rested on the hill-sides, and talked literature. In August the visit was repeated. Hayne con-

[108] Letter to Hayne, April 13, 1867 (in Timrod-Goodwin Collection, South Caroliniana Library). The serial was *Joscelyn.*

In a letter to Rachel Lyons (July 7, 1861; in *Southern Literary Messenger,* II, 605-06, Nov. 1940), Timrod criticized "the 'Beulah' of your friend Miss Evans" as a "very clever work," but without any especial excellence or "any marked originality in the style and characters of the story." He objects particularly that "Beulah's transition from scepticism to Faith is left almost wholly unaccounted for."

For Miss Evans' theory concerning poets, Timrod had only contempt: "I think it would not be difficult to show that Poetry is *not* merely a noble *insanity;* and that the errors and eccentricities of poets have not been *in consequence* of, but *in spite* of the influence of the poetical temperament. In fact, the poet, in his completest development, involves the metaphysician, and is a more sound, wholesome, and perfect human being, than the gravest of those utterers of half-truths who set up as philosophers."

[109] Quoted in Hayne, *op. cit.,* 54.

solidates his account of the two visits, but he describes
Timrod as apostrophizing "twilight in the language of
Wordsworth's sonnet," quoting the Elizabethan dramatist
John Ford and wondering if perhaps he was quoting
Fletcher, memorizing a ballad by Jean Ingelow, and read-
ing Robert Buchanan. In talking about his desire to live to
be "*fifty* or fifty-five," Timrod commented on the picture
of old age given in Charles Reade's *Never Too Late to
Mend?* [110]

Timrod wrote to his sister Emily that "Hayne has plenty
of new books—I suffer from an *embarras de richesses*. It is
hard to tell which to begin first. I distract by insane attempts
to read all at once." [111]

The extent of Timrod's knowledge of classical poetry is
difficult to estimate. His friends thought him deeply if not
widely read; Hayne writes that while Aeschylus revolted
him, he was charmed by Sophocles, revelled in "the elegant
art of Virgil," and never wearied of Horace and Catullus.
J. P. K. Bryan goes even farther, and finds a direct indebtedness to Catullus: "At times there is 'the easy elegance of
Catullus,' always his delight, and a metrical translation of
whose poems he had completed." [112]

[110] *Ibid.*, 54-58. After Timrod's death, Emily wrote to Hayne (May 17,
1870; in Timrod-Goodwin Collection) that Henry had once read to her
some lines from Whittier, "which he had copied while at your house."
Henry Austin (in *The Bookman*, 9:343, June, 1899) thought that some of
Timrod's lines reminded one of Whittier. H. T. Thompson, *Henry Timrod*,
117, says that after Timrod's "The Past" appeared in the *Southern Literary
Messenger* (May, 1850), Whittier praised the poem in a letter to Hayne.
Hayne, *op. cit.*, 21, relates the story without mentioning Whittier's name,
and speaks of the "encouraging effect" of the letter on Timrod.
[111] In Timrod-Goodwin Collection, South Caroliniana Library.
[112] Hayne, *op. cit.*, 18; J. P. K. Bryan, in *Poems*, xxxiii. A former student
of Timrod's who is supposed to have inspired his "Præceptor Amat," Miss
Felicia Robinson, says that Timrod "spent as much of his time as his duties
would allow in reading and studying, and was rarely without some book
in his hand. . . . He was a very learned man, being devoted to the Classics,

If it ever existed in fact, the translation has disappeared. W. A. Courtenay could not locate it, although he believed that Timrod not only had completed the work but had also had it set in type, in the same manner as the poems for an English edition. When he asked Mrs. Lloyd for the proof-sheets of this translation, he got what is possibly the final answer: "I cannot recall that he commenced a metrical version of Catullus, but I have no doubt but that he contemplated doing it at some time . . . I am sure it was never begun." However, she admits in another letter that "I did not preserve all Henry's papers," so her disclaimer is not conclusive.[113]

It is impossible without vague guesswork to trace a direct indebtedness in Timrod's original poetry to that of Catullus. There are similarities of tone and manner, but there is, also, the possibility that these are traceable to an English intermediary.[114] Of Timrod's direct knowledge, no doubt exists.

---

and able to read fluently French, German, Latin and Greek" (quoted in Wauchope, *Henry Timrod*, 12-13). Simms (in *Southern Society*, I: 18, Oct. 12, 1867) wrote: "He was a good Latin scholar, something of a Grecian, and possessed a fair general acquaintance with some of the Continental languages." Henry Austin, *op. cit.*, 342, thinks one line of "A Dedication" is "well-nigh as luscious with liquids as its prototype in Vergil's First Eclogue." H. T. Thompson, *Henry Timrod*, 15, tells of acquiring "a copy of Cooper's Vergil now unfortunately lost, which Timrod had used at school, and which the writer afterwards used. The pages of this old book were embellished with caricatures in pencil, and accompanied with doggerel verses in Timrod's handwriting which embodied pungent and sarcastic criticism of his classmates."

[113] Letters, March 15, 1898, and March 30, 1900, in *Memories of the Timrod Revival 1898-1901* (bound Ms. volume in Charleston Library Society).

[114] Professor Cardwell seems definitely convinced of this. In the Introduction to *Uncollected Poems of Henry Timrod*, 4-5, he notes: "Some possible classic parallels there are. The quatrain *'There is I know not what about thee,'* is of course similar to Martial, I. xxxii (cf. also Catullus, LXXXV): but it is clearly playing upon Brown's famous impromptu translation rather than upon Martial's original. One may compare both 'Sweet

His copy of Catullus is available, and is extensively annotated; it lends support to the statements that Timrod either
translated or intended to translate the poems, for it is the
only one of his extant books that shows numerous notes and
markings. Yet these may reveal only a student's transcrip-
tion from lectures or commentaries. Timrod's notes indicate an interest in poetic metaphor, in idiomatic expression, in variant readings suggested by commentaries, and
in identifying persons and places, especially the Greek and
Latin synonyms for the same name.[115]

On the flyleaf, Timrod has quoted lines of poetry from

----

let not our slanderers' and *'Let V——y prattle'* with Catullus, V, but the
similarities are quite general. For an example of a faint reminiscence of the
Anacreontea, compare Ode 8 (numbering of the Loeb edition) with the
verses *'For high honours.'* For another faint echo of a classic poem, compare *'Six months's such a wonderful time'* with Horace, I, v. Here, as in
the instance of Martial, I. xxxii, mentioned above, an English intermediary
or poem on a similar theme (cf. Suckling's 'Out upon it!') is probably to
be assumed." Peirce Bruns, *op. cit.*, 270, says that "from all Timrod's lighter
verse there breathes gently . . . the faint, sweet perfume of Catullus'
'Dainty Volume,'" and compares Timrod's "A Dedication" with Catullus,
LXXV.

[115] Timrod's pocket-size copy, now in the Charleston Library Society,
included the works of three Latin poets: *Catulli, Tibulli, et Propertii, Opera*
(London, 1822). I give an example of each type of annotation: IV:
utrumque . . . pedem, underscored, with note "The lower corners of the
sails and the ropes by which they were made fast were called *pedes;*" limpi-
dum lacum, underscored, with note, "Lake Benacus." X: caput unctius
referret, "a metaphor for becoming rich." XXXII: meridiatum, "to pass the
noon, to take one's siesta." LI: "Ad Lesbiam," "The first three stanzas of
this poem are translated from Sappho's celebrated ode preserved by
Longinus." LXI: Julia Manlio . . . bona cum bona / Nubit alite virgo,
"Julia will her Manlius wed, / Good with good, a blessed bed. Leigh Hunt."
LXIII: ll. 6-8, "Note the abrupt transition to the feminine gender"; l. 75,
"Condemned as a spurious line by the best commentators." LXXXIX:
omnia plena puellis / Cognatis, "crowds of female cousins—idiomatic as
omnia miseriarum plenissima (Cicero)."

The Tibullus has no marks or notes; the Propertius a few underlinings,
two or three notes on words, and one change in punctuation: I, XX, 32,
"Ah! dolor ibat," to "Ah dolor! ibat."

Ovid, Martial, and François Maynard (in French). They indicate that Timrod considered Catullus' life more virtuous than his writings; the Martial runs, "Lasciva est nobis pagina, vita proba est." And the French verse notes that if the author's pen is evil, his life is decorous. Presumably these quotations seemed appropriate: it may be that Timrod felt some justification or palliation was needed for the more licentious passages.

His copies of Tibullus, Propertius, Cornelius Nepos, and Statius [116] have survived, but they contribute little that is significant beyond the record of his ownership. In spite of the quotation from Ovid on the flyleaf of Catullus, Timrod did not read the entire poem until 1866. In a letter to Hayne, he attacks James Wood Davidson's critical acumen and classical scholarship; to prove that Davidson's knowledge was faulty, he cites a personal experience: "I borrowed from him not long ago a copy of Ovid's Metamorphoses, of which I had hitherto only read fragments in the original. He told me that he had only glanced into it himself and spoke of the difficulty of the Latin. I took the book home and found it perfectly easy Latin for very ordinary scholarship. I read it through with little more trouble than so much English." [117]

A year later, in again commenting on Davidson's ignorance, Timrod gives a little more information on his own reading: "Of Horace he literally knows nothing. I have tried him with several other authors—but he seems to be familiar with none of them. The other day he spoke in raptures of Persius. I had not then read Persius, but curious to see D's taste, I went to the library and glanced over his

[116] *Cornelii Nepotis Vitae* (The Regent's Classics. Pocket Edition. London, 1819); bound in the same volume, *Pomponii Melae, De Situ Orbis, Libri Tres* (London, 1819); *P. Papinii Statii Opera* (London, 1822).
[117] March 7, 1866; quoted in Hubbell, *op. cit.*, 53-54.

Satires." [118] From the lack of enthusiasm implicit in this statement, a glance was apparently enough.

Though he used "Aglaus," the name of a Greek pastoral poet, as an early pseudonym, and though he was certainly conversant with Greek literature, there are no indications of its effect upon him. In "Præceptor Amat," he manages to use a Greek phrase cleverly enough that it fits naturally into the mock-pedantic context, and into the rhyme as well as the rhythm. [119] Likewise, one can only guess at his knowledge of German. His father was proud of his German descent (the name was originally Dimroth), and served as Captain of the German Fusiliers during the Seminole War. The one tangible result of this German blood is a translation, "Song of Mignon," from the *Wilhelm Meister* of Goethe. Apparently Timrod did not consider it worth publishing; Simms speaks of it, justly, as "not worthy of his pen." [120]

A few times Timrod mentions his interest in French. He wrote his sister that his pronunciation was considered "elegant," and he occasionally employs a French phrase in his correspondence. [121] His extant copy of Rousseau's *La Nouvelle Héloïse* has no marginal comments; [122] he does not

[118] Letter to Hayne, March 26, 1867; quoted in Hubbell, *op. cit.*, 76.

[119] In the same poem, Timrod speaks of a "much-valued edition of Homer," and of "the Greek's multitudinous line." Walter Hines Page, in the *South-Atlantic*, I: 367 (March, 1878), writes that "A Mother's Wail" is Timrod's most nearly perfect poem, and to the reader of Simonides seems almost Greek-like.

[120] On W. H. Timrod's war service, see G. A. Cardwell, Jr., "William Henry Timrod, the Charleston Volunteers, and the Defense of St. Augustine," in *North Carolina Historical Review*, XVIII: 27-37, Jan., 1941. The "Song of Mignon" is printed in *Uncollected Poems*, 103-04; Simms' remark is quoted in Hubbell, *op. cit.*, 122 n.

[121] Letter to Emily, July 4, 1851 (in Timrod-Goodwin Collection, South Caroliniana Library). In the letter to Hayne, March 7, 1866, he speaks of Davidson's critical *niaiseries*, which deserve only "a round dozen 'grands coups de pieds dans le derrière.' "

[122] Now in the Timrod Museum at Florence, S. C.

mention the French author in any known letter, or remark on Rousseau's treatment of nature. Yet when he wanted it, Timrod found an apt quotation in French to describe Catullus.

There is a strong and pleasant temptation for any writer on Timrod to play up a father's influence. Every account of William Henry Timrod portrays him as attractive, studious, and independent, an excellent bookbinder who was proud of his craftsmanship, a good citizen and soldier, and an affectionate husband and parent. Although the local newspaper frequently mentioned his name in connection with the activities of the Fusiliers and the German Friendly Society, he clipped for his Daybook only the annual announcement of the officers of the Charleston Library Society; these show him a director from 1827 to 1829.[123] He talked well about literature, and attracted to him the ablest men in Charleston. If his poetry was definitely minor and frequently derivative, it had also a firm craftsmanship and occasional excellence.

In 1814, William Henry Timrod published his one book, *Poems, on Various Subjects.*[124] In his maturer days, he was

[123] See Hayne, *op. cit.*, 8-17, and Hubbell, *op. cit.*, 165-78; Timrod's Daybook, in the Charleston Library Society, has been preserved only for the four years 1825-1829. James McCarter, who employed Timrod for over ten years, wrote to Hayne in 1867: "His wonderful powers of conversation, his genial manner, his pleasant and amiable temper, his exquisite humour, and pungent wit, soon gathered round him a knot of clever young men, who relished his company, and enjoyed his jokes," so that his workshop was called Timrod's Club (Hubbell, *op. cit.*, 173-74). Hayne quotes several of his later poems, including "To Harry."

[124] A tiny volume of 78 pages. The first poem, "Quebec," is subtitled "In Imitation of Campbell's Hohenlinden"; "A Dream" is a weak, conventionalized poet's vision of a "beauteous maid" who vanishes when the poet wakes; "To Pyrrha" has above the title, "Horace, Book I, Ode V, Imitated"; various poems celebrate the charms of such pastoral ladies as Julia, Celia, Thyrsa; on p. 61 the poet calls himself Strephon; several poems are remotely

ashamed of this youthful work, and regretted the publication.[125] Later verses were published in local magazines, and
four of them appear in *The Charleston Book* (1845). This
work reveals that William Timrod had read Moore and
Byron; it shows a maturer mind and a better command of
verse. That Henry was pleased with his father's poems is
easily proved: in 1864, he re-printed several in the *Daily
South Carolinian.*

The elder Timrod died on July 28, 1838, when Henry was
ten years old. Any personal influence was very early in
Henry's life, and cannot be traced in his poetry. Simms, who
knew both father and son, fancied that there was a general
resemblance, but he suggests nothing more: Henry's
"genius was, in some degree, inherited. His father—William
H. Timrod—was a poet before him . . . He wrote freely
and frequently. He published a volume of poems in Charleston, some fifty years ago, the general characteristics of
which somewhat resembled those of his son. He, too, was a
lover of nature, and his poems were meant frequently to
illustrate her phases." [126]

It would also be pleasant, but I believe equally impossible, to find evidence of direct indebtedness to the

---

in the Cavalier tradition, with the air sometimes listed under the title (p. 57,
"Song." / "Air—The Glasses Sparkle on the Board"); a few are sonnets;
"Sullivan's Island" is a didactic poem in heroic couplets. The most interest-
ing, "Noon. An Eclogue" has three negro characters, Sampy, Cudjoe, and
Quashebo; and some negro dialect which the author explains in footnotes.
The poem is a deliberate mixture of dialect and high-flown language; two
women who are talked about are Clarissa and Jemimah. Many of the blank
pages of the Daybook contain later poems.

[125] Hubbell, *op. cit.*, 166: "In an undated letter Emily Timrod Goodwin
wrote to Hayne: 'I heard him regret deeply that he had ever allowed them
to appear in print, so meanly did he think of them.' "

[126] W. G. Simms, in *Southern Society*, I: 18-19, Oct. 12, 1867; quoted
in Hubbell, *op. cit.*, 155.

Charleston writers of his day. The men who with Hugh Swinton Legaré wrote the distinguished papers in the *Southern Review* were no longer active, but the group that congregated at Russell's Bookshop and Simms' town house had wit and intelligence. Simms, James Mathewes Legaré, S. Henry Dickson, John Dickson Bruns, and several others wrote capable and occasionally distinguished verse; Petigru, Grayson, Russell, and similar men had taste and energetic opinions. To them all, literature was alive. These doctors, lawyers, merchants, and writers talked heatedly yet intelligently of books and ideas; they had magazines at hand to publish their shorter work when, and if, they got around to putting it on paper.[127]

To the younger men, this intellectual atmosphere was bracing. They considered themselves an integral part of an active group, working in the tradition of English poetry yet contributing something new and individual. Timrod, Hayne and Bruns, the classicists della Torre and Gildersleeve, and other young men talked freely with each other; undoubtedly, each profited by the criticism of the others.[128] Inevitably, the tension of increasing bitterness directed their thoughts from literature to immediate political and eco-

[127] For a vivid account of this group, see P. H. Hayne, "Ante-Bellum Charleston," in *The Southern Bivouac*, I: 327-36, Nov. 1885.

[128] Unfortunately, no record of this criticism exists, except in the writings of Hayne and Bruns on Timrod. Yates Snowden ("A Reminiscence of Henry Timrod," Charleston *News and Courier*, Dec. 20, 1903) tells of one gathering of five young men: Timrod, Bruns, John della Torre, William A. Martin, and the unnamed narrator. Bruns claimed that della Torre had discovered the Latin original of a recent poem of Timrod's; della Torre read as the original his own translation into 13th century Latin. Timrod, nonplussed, protested innocence until the other men laughed at him and admitted the hoax. Years later, Rachel Lyons Heustis remembered especially Timrod's "entire absence of jealousy or unkind criticism of contemporary poets," and his willingness to listen to criticism of his own verse (letter to W. A. Courtenay, March 20, 1899, in *Memories of the Timrod Revival 1898-1901*).

nomic problems; the war itself disrupted their lives. Each writer was forced to develop his powers alone, and under difficulties.

Timrod knew an intellectual and personal loneliness. Physical weakness prevented him from taking an active part in the war. These personal deprivations are not expressed in his poems, but they helped to add intensity and strength to his work. Only through his writing could he become identified with the thought and emotion of his region. This, at least, he achieved. His opportunity for meditation, for development, for an expression in poetry of his own critical ideals, was cut short by poverty and death.

The Character and Scope of the Sonnet[1]

lıllllllllllllllllllllllllllllllllllllllllllllllllll

THE sonnet has never been a popular form of verse. Those who maintain that the poet should address himself to the popular heart alone, may regard this as a significant fact. We are not, however, so disposed to consider it. As far as we know anything of that interesting organ, the popular heart understands very little about poetry, and cares less. The audience of the poet, "fit, though few," [2] is even more limited than that of the musician. As there are a great many persons wholly unable to enjoy the music of an overture, or an opera, so there are a still greater number who are equally incompetent to appreciate an epic or a sonnet. We appeal to the experience of every earnest lover and true critic of poetry. How often have his sensibilities been shocked while reading to divers representatives of this popular heart, some noble passage which has stirred his own soul to its very depth. The subtle melody has fallen on deaf ears. The deep thought, the lofty imagination have not been comprehended at all. "Very good, I dare say, but— I am no critic," or, "quite pretty, but after all, give me a song of Moore's." The enthusiastic reader shuts the book with an internal malediction. In truth, we are not inclined to regard this popular heart as a human heart at all. It is only a mean, narrow, unintelligent thing, which beats some-

61

times under fine broadcloth, and sometimes under coarser textures, to the tune of dollars and cents. Where, since the time of Milton, has the reputation of every poet, with the single exception of Burns, commenced? Not with the multitude. A few cultivated persons explain their admiration to the popular heart, which echoes it much as an empty room echoes a voice. Even the popularity of the songs of Burns and Moore we are disposed to attribute rather to the airs to which they have been married than to the excellence of their poetry.

It is not our object, in this essay, to argue the sonnet into popularity. The attempt would be not less absurd than that of the foolish fellow who tried to teach an ape to read. We only design to answer some of the objections urged against this form of verse by people who should know better. There is Rogers. That complacent poet has remarked that "he had never attempted to write a sonnet, as he could see no reason why a man, who had anything to say, should be tied down to fourteen lines." [3] He adds, somewhat condescendingly, that it "did very well for Wordsworth, as its strict limits prevented him from lapsing into that diffuseness to which he was prone." That a poet who was wont to confine himself to four couplets a day, as much we suspect from actual sterility in word and thought, as with any design of polishing his verse, should speak in terms of such cool disparagement of the style of Wordsworth, is amusing enough. But with the banker's strictures upon the author of Laodamia, we have nothing to do. What shall we say in reply to that objection which turns upon the impossibility of compressing the thoughts of Mr. Rogers within the compass of fourteen lines. The answer lies in a nutshell. It is plain that Mr. Rogers had never reflected upon the nature of the sonnet. He did not know that it partakes—with certain differences which will be soon alluded to—of the nature of a stanza. We can give no reason wherefore, in the spenserian stanza, the verse should always, and the sense generally conclude with the ninth line, except that the nice ear of the poet, by whom it was invented, so determined it. The poets who followed the inventor finding the stanza to be one of great variety, sweetness and strength, adopted it, without inquiring why it might not consist of eight or ten lines. In the same manner, the sonnet was the invention of some other poet of happy taste; and this little harp of fourteen strings, after having been swept with great effect by the hands of a few great masters, has been accepted and approved as one of the legitimate instruments of poetry. There are certain ears on which music of every kind—Mozart's as well as Milton's—can fall only in parts; and to such ears it is not surprising that no sufficient reason can be given why the sonnet should never transgress or fall short of the limits which have been assigned it. But the educated poetical ear, capable of appreciating the music of the sonnet as a whole, will detect in it a strain of melody, which, like an air that has been played out, comes naturally and easily to a close at the fourteenth line. We do not say that this effect is always produced, but it will be always produced whenever the sonnet is properly written. And the poet who complains of the shackles that bind him, lacks either skill or genius.

An objection will be suggested to the above remarks by that which constitutes the difference between the sonnet and the stanza. The latter often leaves the sense incomplete, and may run into a succeeding stanza; while the sonnet, even when used as the stanza of a long poem, (as in Wordsworth's poem on the river Duddon, and in his ecclesiastical sonnets,) must be at the same time a complete poem in itself. This objection is of course no answer to what we have urged as to the musical effect of the sonnet as a stanza, but points only to the additional trammels which it imposes on the poet. That it does impose such additional trammels we acknowledge at once. But what then? The poet finds ready made to his hand, an air of exquisite sweetness to which he may set his thought, and to which, if he possesses the due degree of skill, he may, by means of pause and cadence, give the most delightful variations without destroying or marring the effect of the original melody. Must he refuse to employ it simply because it is difficult? That many poets have written bad sonnets only proves a difficulty which nobody denies, and which those poets had not the ability to overcome.

It is not long since we heard the law of the sonnet ascribed to the same caprice which once led men to write verses in the shape of triangles and other geometrical figures. That that law depends upon something more than caprice, we think we have already said enough to show. But the remark could scarcely have been made in earnest. No apology whatever could be forged, by the most ingenious critic, which could justify in the slightest degree the freaks of pedantry alluded to. But it will not be denied that the sonnet admits at least of a very plausible defence. No good poetry that we have ever heard of has been pressed into the figure of a trapezoid. But it will not be denied that much noble poetry has been given to the world through the medium of the sonnet.

The sonnet has been called artificial. It *is* artificial, but only as all forms of verse are artificial. There are persons who imagine poetry to be the result of a sort of mystical inspiration, scarcely to be subjected to the bounds of space and time. Others regarding it as the outgushing of a present emotion, cannot conceive how the poet, carried on by the "divine afflatus," should always contrive to rein in his Pegasus at a certain goal. All this is simply ridiculous. If the poet have his hour of inspiration (though we are so sick of the cant of which this word has been the fruitful source, that we dislike to use it) it is not during the act of composition. A distinction must be made between the moment when the great thought first breaks upon the mind,

> ———————"leaving in the brain
> A rocking and a ringing," [4]

and the hour of patient and elaborate execution. It is in the conception only that the poet is the *vates*. In the labor of putting that conception into words, he is simply the artist. A great poet has defined poetry to be "emotion recollected in tranquility." [5] No man with grief in his heart, could sit straightway down to strain that grief through iambics. No man, exulting in a delirium of joy, ever bubbles in anapaests. Were this so, the poet would be the most wonderful of improvisators; and, perhaps, poetry would be no better than what improvisations usually are. There can be no doubt that much of the most passionate verse in the English, or any other language, has been

"Thoughtfully fitted to the Orphean lyre." [6]

The act of composition is indeed attended with an emotion peculiar to itself, and to the poet; and this emotion is sufficient of itself to give a glow and richness to the poet's language; yet, it leaves him at the same time in such command of his faculties that he is able to choose his words almost as freely, though by no means so deliberately, as the painter chooses his colors. We are inclined to think that the emotion of the poet somewhat resembles in its metaphysical

character, those inexplicable feelings with which we all witness a tragic performance on the stage—feelings which,
even while they rend the heart, are always attended by a
large amount of vivid pleasure.

It would be easy to multiply quotations in confirmation of
our remarks. Wordsworth speaks of himself as

> "Not used to make
> A present joy the matter of his song;" [7]

and Matthew Arnold separates, as we have separated, "the
hour of insight" from the hour of labor.

> "We cannot kindle when we will,
>   The fire that in the heart resides,
> The spirit bloweth and is still,
>   In mystery our soul abides:
> *But tasks in hours of insight willed*
> *May be through hours of gloom fulfilled.*" [8]

Is it not also a significant fact that the best loved verses
have been written by men who, at the time of writing them,
had long passed that age during which love is warmest, and
the heart most susceptible? The songs of Moore's middle
age are far superior to the Anacreontics of his passionate
youth.

We confess we are unable to see the stigma conveyed in
the term artificial, as applied to the sonnet. The poet is an
artist, and, we suppose, he regards every sort of stanza but
as the artificial mould into which he pours his thought. The
very restriction so much complained of, he knows to be, in
some respects, an advantage. It forces him to condensation;
and if it sometimes induces a poetaster to stretch a thought
to the finest tenuity, what argument is that against the
sonnet? As well might Jones object to the violin of Paganini,
because his neighbor Smith is a wretched fiddler.

The sonnet is designed, as it is peculiarly fitted for the development of a single thought, emotion, or picture. It is governed by another law not less imperative than that which determines its length. This law the cavillers have not as yet interfered with, doubtless, because they know nothing of its existence. Yet, perhaps, it is that which constitutes the chief difficulty in the composition of the sonnet. We do not know how else to characterize it but as the law of unity. In a poem made up of a series of stanzas, the thought in the first stanza suggests the thought in the second, and both may be equally important. The concluding stanza may have wandered as far in its allusions from the opening stanza, as the last from the first sentence in an essay. In other words, the poet has the liberty of rambling somewhat, if his fancy so dispose him. In the sonnet this suggestive progress from one thought to another is inadmissible. It must consist of one leading idea, around which the others are grouped for purposes of illustration only. Most of the sonnets of Wordsworth meet this requirement exactly. Whatever be the number of the images they contain, they are usually perfect in the unity of the impression which they leave upon the mind of the reader.

At some future time we shall return to this subject, and passing by many cavils equally as trivial as those we have discussed, we will examine and illustrate more fully the laws which govern this department of verse. At present we will only say that we claim for it a proud distinction, as it is represented in English literature. We believe that we could gather from it a greater body of tersely expressed and valuable thought, than from any equal quantity of those fugitive verses, the laws of which are less exacting. It abounds in those "great thoughts, grave thoughts," [9] which, embodied in lines of wonderful pregnancy, haunt the memory forever.

Brief as the sonnet is, the whole power of a poet has some-times been exemplified within its narrow bounds, as com-pletely as within the compass of an epic. Thought is inde-pendent of space, and it would hardly be an exaggeration to say that the poet—the minister of thought—enjoys an equal independence. To-day his "stature reaches the sky," [10] to-morrow he will shut himself up in the bell of a tulip, or the cup of a lily.

What is Poetry?[1]

ııııuıuıuııuıuıuuııuuıuııuuıuuıuuıuuıuuıuuıuıu

THERE are certain operations of the human mind upon itself and the world without, which, when they take form and body in language, have been denominated Poetry. To describe the nature of these operations, in a single definition, has long been the aim of the philosophical critic. No perfectly satisfactory definition has yet been attained. We could quote a score, gathered from different sources—all more or less wide of the mark. As we recall them, we are reminded of a childish search once actually commenced by ourselves, after the pot of gold which is said to lie buried at the foot of the rainbows.

A writer in the July number of this Magazine has attempted to settle the question.

By very improperly making poetry the antithesis of prose (prose, as Coleridge justly observes,[2] being properly opposed only to metre), and by confounding the subjective with the objective of poetry, he has arrived, with some plausibility, at what he offers us as a definition of poetry. It is, in reality, an extremely poor *dictionary* definition of a poem.

The truth is, the writer has altogether mistaken the question. That question is, as we have already implied, not how to define the forms of poetry, nor how to distinguish poetry from prose (the philosophic critic would as soon think of

69

contrasting a virtue with a colour), but what is that element in human nature—what, we repeat, are those operations of the human faculties, which, when *incarnated* in language, are generally recognized as poetry.

The theory of the writer is, that poetry is a mere synonym for a composition in verse. Hence, the general dissatisfaction occasioned by his article—a dissatisfaction which we have heard expressed by many who, displeased they scarcely knew why, and dimly conscious of the true faith, were yet unable to find, in their own undefined notions, a logical refutation of the heresy. The genuine lovers of poetry *feel* that its essential characteristics underlie the various forms which it assumes. Ask any man of sensibility to define poetry, and he will endeavor to convey to you some idea, vague, doubtless, and shadowy, of that which, in his imagination, constitutes its spirit. The few poets who have attempted to solve the question, have looked rather into themselves than into the poems which they have written. One describes poetry as "emotion recollected in tranquility;" another, as "the recollection of the best and happiest hours of the best and happiest minds." [3] These definitions— if definitions they can be called—are inadequate enough;— but they indicate, correctly, we think, the direction in which the distinctive principle of poetry is to be sought.

It is time that we should place the argument which we are discussing before the reader. We shall, perhaps, omit a passage here and there, but the reader has only to turn to the July number of this Magazine to see the argument *in extenso:*

"What is Poetry?

"It will help us in knowing what it is, to determine first what it is not. It is not the nature of the thoughts expressed that makes a *book* a *poem*. It is not beauty of imagery, nor play of fancy, nor creative power of imagination, nor expression of emotion or passion, nor delineation of character, nor force, refinement or purity of language, that constitutes the *distinctive quality of poetry*. Because it is evident that there are passages in prose capable of being compared, in all these properties, not disadvantageously, with the noblest productions of the ancient or modern muse. Take for an example of beautiful imagery, the often quoted passage from Milton's Tractate on Education, where he expatiates on the delights of learning: 'I will lead you to a hill-side, laborious, indeed, on the first ascent, but else so smooth, so green, so full of goodly prospects and melodious sounds on every side, that the harp of Orpheus was not more charming;' or Burke's eulogy on the adventurous hardihood of the seamen of America, or his description of the French Queen, &c.

"Where, in poetry, shall we find invention, fancy, imagination, more abundantly exhibited than in the writings of Defoe, or Fielding, or Scott, or Dickens? ° ° ° And yet, unless it be metaphorically to sustain a theory, no one calls Tom Jones, or Robinson Crusoe, or Ivanhoe, *a poem*."

Then follow two quotations from the Bible, which, in spite of the sublimity of the one, and the beauty of the other, are pronounced (and we make no dangerous admission in saying very properly pronounced) to be "prose, nevertheless."

"A prose translation of the Iliad, containing every sentiment and description, faithfully expressed, *would not be a poem*. The passage from Milton, if turned into his own sonorous verse, would be *as genuine poetry* as the Comus or Paradise Lost. Turned into metrical form, by the commonest hand even, the prose is changed into *poetry*, the words remaining the same:

> "We lead your footsteps to a mountain side
> Laborious on the first ascent, but else
> So smooth, so green, so full of goodly sights,
> And sounds melodious, that the harp itself
> Or song of Orpheus, not more charming seemed."

"But if it is not the thought, sentiment or imagery, either grand or beautiful, that makes the *distinctive quality of poetry*, what is it that does? If the distinguishing property be not in the substance, it must be *in the form of the work;* if not in the conceptions, it must be in the words that express them.

"But the words of a language are common to prose and poetry.

"It must be, then, in the form of arranging words that we find the peculiar something that *constitutes poetry.*"

With a few more remarks, not very material to the argument, the writer concludes that poetry may be defined "as the expression, by words, of thought or emotion, in conformity with metrical and rythmical laws."

The sophistry of this argument lies principally in a very illogical confusion of the ideas conveyed by the terms *poem,* and *poetry.* The italics, which are our own, are meant to call the attention of the reader to the repeated change from one term to the other, as if they were identical in signification.—The writer would have us infer that because it is impossible to call Ivanhoe a poem, it must follow that it does not contain a single element of poetry. And in a passage which we have not quoted, he seems to insist that because "no one can deny that the work of Lucretius is a poem;" we are, therefore, to infer that, from the beginning to the end, it is all poetry. We shall endeavor soon to show the absurdity of these conclusions, if, indeed, this simple statement be not all that is necessary to condemn them.

The reader ought also to observe, without our aid, that the writer sets out with the notion tacitly, though perhaps unconsciously assumed, that poetry is just what his definition describes it to be, that his definition is implied and taken for granted in the very arguments by which he reaches it—in a word, that his whole train of reasoning is but a simple *petitio principii*. For it is plain that, unless we accept his definition of poetry, or one no less narrow, it is impossible to recognize that antithesis of prose to poetry on which the whole argument is based. It is equally plain that, without recognizing that antithesis, it is impossible to see any force in those arguments drawn from the fact that there are to be found in prose, passages equal in point of "fancy, passion, or imagination," to many noble passages in verse.

Do we speak literally, or (as this writer avers, drawing, we admit, a legitimate inference from his own definition) are we employing a mere figure of speech, when we commend a passage of prose, teeming with passion and imagination, as true and genuine poetry?

Before answering this question, we must be permitted to say something as to our conclusions on the nature of poetry. We shall not pretend to give the reader an adequate definition. Our purpose in this essay is not to establish a theory of our own, but simply to expose the falsehood and superficiality of the one before us.

Coleridge remarks that the question, What is poetry? is very nearly the same with, What is a poet? [4] The distinctive qualities of poetry grow out of the poetic genius itself.

The ground of the poetic character is a more than ordinary sensibility. Other qualifications, indeed, are necessary to complete our idea of the poet, but for the ends of our argument, it will be necessary to consider this one alone. From this characteristic of the poet results what we regard as an essential characteristic of poetry,—a characteristic which should be left out of no definition; we refer to the medium of strong emotion, through which poetry looks at its objects, and in which, to borrow a chemical metaphor of Arthur Hallam's, it "holds them all fused." [5] Hence, again, is derived a third peculiarity in the *language* of poetry, which, with a difference in the degree, not the kind of its force, arising from an imagination more than usually vivid, is the language natural to men in a state of excitement, is sensuous, picturesque, and impassioned.[6]

It is, in fact, only when we come to speak of the language, or of the forms of poetry, that we are moving in the same plane of argument with the writer. What distinguishes the language of poetry? The writer maintains that it is the metrical and rythmical arrangement of the words. We, on the contrary, are disposed to think it is the character of the language itself.

One of the members upon which the writer's faulty syllogism is made to rest, is the following statement: "The words of a language are common to poetry and prose." This needs considerable qualification.

Nothing is better known to the poet than the fact that prose and verse have each a vocabulary of their own. Words, and even forms of expression, are still used in verse which are considered obsolete by the prose-writer. On the other hand, verse rejects a large number of words which are part of the legitimate stock of prose. Among these are most of the long words in the English tongue. Why are they rejected? Simply on account of their metrical impracticability? That, doubtless, is a good reason for excluding them from verse, but why does poetry endorse that exclusion—what constitutes their unfitness to express the passions and emotions of poetry? The answer is easy. Poetry does not deal in pure abstractions. However abstract be his thought, the poet is compelled, by his passion-fused imagination, to give it life, form, or color. Hence the necessity of employing the sensuous, or concrete words of the language; and hence the exclusion of long words, which in English are nearly all purely and austerely abstract, from the poetic vocabulary. Whenever a poet drags a number of these words into his verse, we say that he is prosaic; and by this we mean, not that he has written prose (for verse can never be prose), nor that he is simply deficient in spirit and vivacity, as this writer implies, but that he has not used the legitimate language of poetry; he has written something which is only distinguished from the ordinary dead-level of unimpassioned prose by the feet upon which it crawls. In the course of our poetical reading, we have seen the employment of a single abstract word impart to a line all the effect of prose. An instance occurs to us at this moment, but as it is taken from the writings of a poet very near home, we forbear to quote it.

We must not be understood to say that abstract words and abstract thinking are the sole sources of the prosaic. A passage may be rendered prosaic by a phrase not itself abstract in word or meaning, which has been made commonplace by constant repetition. But such a phrase will generally be found to have lost, with its novelty, the *picturesqueness* which it at first possessed. It no longer calls up the image which it expresses, it merely suggests the thought which it stands for, and affects the mind in exactly the same manner as the boldest abstraction.

If verse may sometimes be prosaic, prose may sometimes be poetic. Poetry is a subtle spirit, and appears in different guises, and in various places. In prose, indeed,

> "Her delights
> Are dolphin-like, and show themselves above
> The element they sport in;" [7]

yet, even in that domain, her movements are at times scarcely less free and graceful than when she is floating through the Heaven of Song.

It is a characteristic of poetry in its aim to create beauty, that it levies, for this purpose, its contributions on every side. Not content, as the ordinary prose-writer *should be*, with such words as are simply the most proper to express the meaning to be conveyed, it seeks also the most beautiful— the sound, and the associations connected with a word, being taken into consideration as well as the sense. The words of poetry, without interfering with the general effect, challenge a slight attention to themselves. This is what Coleridge meant when he described poetry as "the best words in the best order." [8]

When, therefore, we meet with a passage of prose, which, while it is kindled into eloquence by the beauty which it strives to embody, seems also to be revelling in its own, and the language of which is sensuous, picturesque and passionate, we may with perfect justice pronounce that passage to be poetry. Many such passages are to be found in the writings of Milton, and of Jeremy Taylor.

> "I looked upon a plain of green,
>   That some one called the land of prose,
> Where many living things were seen
>   In movement or repose.

"I looked upon a stately hill,
    That well was named the Mount of Song,
Where golden shadows dwelt at will,
    The woods and streams among.

"But most this fact my wonder bred,
    Though known by all the nobly wise,
It was the mountain streams that fed
    The fair green plain's amenities." ° [9]

We are inclined to agree with the writer, in refusing the title of a just *poem* to any work which is not metrical in form. Yet we respect the opinions of those who maintain that there may be such a thing as a prose-poem. Doubtless, much could be said in support of those opinions. But such is the avidity of poetry in gathering up its materials for the creation of beauty, so necessary does it seem that its language should possess every charm of which language is capable, that it appears to demand verse as its natural and proper expression. Moreover, those who are disposed to agree with us in our views of poetry, will see that no poem, no long poem at least, can be (Coleridge says it ought not to be) all poetry. [10] Whether a poem be narrative, or philosophical, there will be parts and aspects of its subject wholly insusceptible of genuine poetic treatment. Verse, therefore, is required to preserve these parts in some sort of keeping with the poetry, the object being the production of a harmonious whole.

The reader now holds in his hand the key to all the sophistical arguments of the writer. He will see that while we acknowledge the work of Lucretius to be a poem, we may yet declare that much of it is not poetry. He will see, also, that without denying the passage from Milton's Tractate on Education to be prose, we may yet assert that it contains

° Sterling.

the genuine elements of poetry. And so on with all the rest of the writer's various illustrations.

The writer speaks much about logical precision, and the confusion into which this subject has been thrown by a misconception of what he chooses to term the figurative expressions of poetic prose, and prosaic verse. The real source of this confusion is the opposition of poetry to prose. For this relation of the two to each other, the writer may indeed urge the precedent of common usage, and the practice of many good writers.—But the impropriety was exposed long ago by Coleridge and Wordsworth,[11] and we hardly expected to see it repeated at this date in the pages of Russell's Magazine.

Much of the article we have been examining is consumed in illustrating the profound truth that tastes differ. They do, indeed. There must be a vast difference between the taste of a man who regards the Ancient Mariner as the noblest of all ballads, and the taste of another who has read through that poem with no other sensation than what is vulgarly termed a turning of the stomach. Of the comments upon this strange, weird production of Coleridge, we shall remark little more than that they seem to us to be conceived very much in the spirit of Charles Lamb's literal Scotchman.[12] And in regard to the assertion that the poem is an offence against a principle of Coleridge himself—Coleridge having said that every poem should be common sense, at least [13]— we may be permitted to suggest it as not impossible that, between the poet's philosophical notion of common sense, and this writer's, there were few points of resemblance. Coleridge certainly did not refer to that quibbling common sense which would apply to a supernatural story,—much the same sort of logic that is resorted to by papas, when they endeavor to prove to the satisfaction of little boys the non-existence of ghosts.

Of the caricature of Wordsworth it is difficult to speak without indignation.

We had once a conversation with a prosaic friend of ours upon the subject of poetry. After pronouncing the whole tribe of poets to be a set of conceited coxcombs, our friend added that he was sure no poet could "truly enjoy the beauties of Nature. The fellows can't look at a sunset without thinking of the fine things which might be said about it." We said nothing, for our friend would not have understood us, if we had told him that a man who looked at a sunset in such a spirit, was not, and could not be, a poet. Yet such was the spirit in which, according to this writer, Wordsworth was accustomed to look at Nature. No one, at all familiar with the writings of Wordsworth, would have made this accusation; and we cannot help suspecting that it is based upon a perusal of the titles of the poems, rather than of the poems themselves. For passage after passage might be adduced, so wholly incompatible with the character assigned to Wordsworth, that, for the sake of the writer's taste and common sense, we must conclude that he knew nothing at all about them.

Perhaps no poet ever felt so deeply, certainly none has ever described so admirably, that complete abandonment of the soul to the influences of Nature, in which

"Thought is not; in enjoyment it expires." [14]

Take the following lines, from the poem composed near Tintern Abbey:

------"Nature then
To me was all in all. I cannot paint
What then I was. The sounding cataract
Haunted me like a passion; the tall rock,

> The mountain, and the deep and gloomy wood,
> Their colours and their forms, were then to me
> An appetite; *a feeling and a love*
> *That had no need of a remoter charm*
> *By thought supplied, or any interest*
> *Unborrowed from the eye.*"

And who will believe that the passage which follows these lines—transcendental though it may be—could be the production of a coxcomb, who traded with Nature for his poetry? In what fitting language it depicts those moods of ecstatic contemplation, in which the soul, through a faculty not dependent upon the senses, feels the presence of that mysterious and universal principle, of which the world is a manifestation!

> "And I have felt
> A presence that disturbs me with the joy
> Of elevated thoughts: a sense sublime
> Of something far more deeply interfused.
> Whose dwelling is the light of setting suns,
> And the round ocean, and the living air,
> And the blue sky, and in the mind of man:
> A motion and a spirit that impels
> All thinking things, all objects of all thought,
> And rolls through all things."

It is useless to multiply quotations to prove the groundlessness of a charge which we can scarcely believe was made in earnest. A few more remarks as to what seems to us an unfair use of the authority of Coleridge, and we have done.

Coleridge has charged upon certain portions of the poems of Wordsworth, "*a matter-of-factness,*" by which he meant an occasional, and somewhat superfluous, minuteness of detail.[15] The fault is probably to be traced to a too great desire, on the part of the poet, to bring the groupings and situations of his few characters distinctly before the mind of the reader. The writer insidiously represents this charge as a general one; and in attempting to account for the blemish, he caricatures in the grossest manner the lofty sense which Wordsworth ever entertained of his office as a poet, and his loving and life-long devotion to its duties.—The whole is so strikingly unjust, that we shall not take the trouble to argue the point.

Coleridge has elsewhere done ample justice to Wordsworth's powers of imaginative description. And Ruskin has pronounced him to be the great poetic landscape painter of the age.

We should like the writer to point out anything like "a matter-of-factness" in the description of the breaking up of the storm in the second book of the Excursion; in the description of the "twin mountain brethren," as seen from the cottage of the Solitary; in the sonnet on Westminster Bridge; in the sonnets, "Methought I saw the footsteps of a Throne," "It is a beauteous evening, calm and free," and "The world is too much with us;" in the blank verse entitled a Night Piece; in the poem on Yew Trees (than the greater part of which, it is impossible to conceive anything further removed from matter-of-fact); in the Ode on the Intimations of Immortality; in the burst which concludes the Song at the Feast of Brougham Castle, and the exquisite quatrains which close that poem; in the Danish Boy; in the Boy of Winandermere; in the stanzas commencing, "Three years she grew in sun and shower;" in the character of the poet as sketched in A Poet's Epitaph; in the austere and spiritual grandeur of Laodamia; or (we are getting out of breath) in the following italicised line of enchanted and enchanting beauty—a whole fairy poem in itself, and alone sufficient to absolve Wordsworth of this charge against him—with which, whether abruptly or not, we shall conclude our article:

> "That tall fern
> So stately, of the queen Osmunda named,
> Plant lovelier, in its own retired abode,
> On Grasmere's beach, than Naiad by the side
> Of Grecian brook, or *Lady of the Mere,*
> *Lone-sitting by the shores of old Romance.*" [16]

Literature in the South[1]

iiiiiiiiiiiiiiiiiiiiiiiiiiiiiiiiiiiiiiiiiiiiiiiiii

WE THINK that at no time, and in no country, has the position of an author been beset with such peculiar difficulties
as the Southern writer is compelled to struggle with from
the beginning to the end of his career. In no country in
which literature has ever flourished has an author obtained
so limited an audience. In no country, and at no period that
we can recall, has an author been constrained by the indifference of the public amid which he lived, to publish with a
people who were prejudiced against him. It would scarcely
be too extravagant to entitle the Southern author the Pariah
of modern literature. It would scarcely be too absurd if
we should compare his position to that of the drawer of
Shakspeare, who stands in a state of ludicrous confusion
between the calls of Prince Hal upon the one side and of
Poins upon the other.[2] He is placed, in fact, much in the
same relation to the public of the North and the public of
the South, as we might suppose a statesman to occupy who
should propose to embody in one code a system of laws
for two neighbouring people, of one of which he was a
constituent, and who yet altogether differed in character,
institutions and pursuits. The people among whom the
statesman lived would be very indignant upon finding, as
they would be sure to find, that some of their interests had

been neglected. The people for whom he legislated at a distance would be equally indignant upon discovering, as they would [be] sure to fancy they discovered, that not one of their interests had received proper attention. Both parties would probably unite, with great cordiality and patriotism, in consigning the unlucky statesman to oblivion or the executioner. In precisely the same manner fares the poor scribbler who has been so unfortunate as to be born South of the Potomac. He publishes a book. It is the settled conviction of the North that genius is indigenous there, and flourishes only in a Northern atmosphere. It is the equally firm conviction of the South that genius—literary genius, at least—is an exotic that will not flower on a Southern soil. Probably the book is published by a Northern house. Straightway all the newspapers of the South are indignant that the author did not choose a Southern printer, and address himself more particularly to a Southern community. He heeds their criticism, and of his next book,—published by a Southern printer—such is the secret though unacknowledged prejudice against Southern authors—he finds that more than one half of a small edition remains upon his hands. Perhaps the book contains a correct and beautiful picture of our peculiar state of society. The North is inattentive or abusive, and the South unthankful, or, at most, indifferent. Or it may happen to be only a volume of noble poetry, full of those universal thoughts and feelings which speak, not to a particular people, but to all mankind. It is censured at the South as not sufficiently Southern in spirit, while at the North it is pronounced a very fair specimen of Southern commonplace. Both North and South agree with one mind to condemn the author and forget his book.

We do not think that we are exaggerating the embarrassments which surround the Southern writer. It cannot be

denied that on the surface of newspaper and magazine
literature there have lately appeared signs that his claims
to respect are beginning to be acknowledged. But, in spite
of this, we must continue to believe, that among a large
majority of Southern readers who devour English books
with avidity, there still exists a prejudice—conscious or un-
conscious—against the works of those authors who have
grown up among themselves. This prejudice is strongest,
indeed, with a class of persons whose opinions do not find
expression in the public prints; but it is on that account more
harmful in its evil and insidious influence. As an instance,
we may mention that it is not once, but a hundred times,
that we have heard the works of the first of Southern
authors [3] alluded to with contempt by individuals who had
never read anything beyond the title-pages of his books.
Of this prejudice there is an easy, though not a very flatter-
ing, explanation.

The truth is, it must be confessed, that though an educated, we are a provincial, and not a highly cultivated
people. At least, there is among us a very general want of a
high critical culture. The principles of that criticism, the
basis of which is a profound psychology, are almost utterly
ignored. There are scholars of pretension among us, with
whom Blair's Rhetoric [4] is still an unquestionable authority.
There are schools and colleges in which it is used as a text-
book. With the vast advance that has been made in critical
science since the time of Blair few seem to be intimately acquainted. The opinions and theories of the last century are
still held in reverence. Here Pope is still regarded by many
as the most *correct* of English poets, and here, Kaimes,[5]
after having been everywhere else removed to the top
shelves of libraries, is still thumbed by learned professors
and declamatory sophomores. Here literature is still re-

garded as an epicurean amusement; not as a study, at least equal in importance, and certainly not inferior in difficulty, to law and medicine. Here no one is surprised when some fossil theory of criticism, long buried under the ruins of an exploded school, is dug up, and discussed with infinite gravity by gentlemen who know Pope and Horace by heart, but who have never read a word of Wordsworth or Tennyson, or who have read them with suspicion, and rejected them with superciliousness.

In such a state of critical science, it is no wonder that we are prudently cautious in passing a favourable judgment upon any new candidates for our admiration. It is no wonder that while we accept without a cavil books of English and Northern reputation, we yet hesitate to acknowledge our own writers, until, perhaps, having been commended by English or Northern critics, they present themselves to us with a "certain alienated majesty." There is another class of critics among us—if critics they can be called—which we must not pass over. This class seem disposed to look upon literature as they look upon a Bavarian sour-krout, a Strasbourg paté, or a New Zealand cutlet of "cold clergyman." It is a mere matter of taste. Each one feels himself at liberty to exalt the author—without reference to his real position in the world of letters, as settled by a competent tribunal— whose works afford *him* the most amusement. From such a principle, of course, the most fantastic and discordant opinions result. One regards that fanciful story, the Culprit Fay of Drake, as the greatest of American poems; and another is indignant if Tennyson be mentioned in the same breath with Longfellow. Now, it is good to be independent; but it is not good to be too independent. Some respect is certainly due to the authority of those who, by a careful and loving study of literature, have won the right to speak *ex cathedra.* Nor is that independence, but license, which is not founded upon a wide and deep knowledge of critical science, and upon a careful and respectful collation of our own conclusions, with the impartial philosophical conclusions of others.

In the course of these remarks, we have alluded to three classes of critics, the bigot, the slave, and we cannot better characterize the third, than as the autocratic. There is yet a fourth, which feels, or professes to feel, a warm interest in Southern literature, and which so far is entitled to our respect. But, unfortunately, the critical principles of this class are quite as shallow as those of any of the others; and we notice it chiefly to expose the absurdity of one of its favourite opinions, adopted from a theory which some years ago arose at the North, and which bore the name of Americanism in literature. After the lapse of a period commensurate with the distance it had to travel, it reached the remote South, where it became, with an intensity of absurdity which is admirable indeed, Southernism in literature.[6] Now, if the theory had gone to the depth of that which constitutes true nationality, we should have no objections to urge against it. But to the understandings of these superficial critics, it meant nothing more than that an author should confine himself in the choice of his subjects to the scenery, the history, and the traditions of his own country. To be an American novelist, it was sufficient that a writer should select a story, in which one half the characters should be backwoodsmen, who talked bad Saxon, and the other half should be savages, who talked Choctaw translated into very bombastic English. To be an American poet, it was sufficient either in a style and measure imitated from Pope and Goldsmith, or in the more modern style and measure of Scott and Wordsworth, to describe the vast prairies of the West, the swamps and pine forests of the South, or the great lakes and broad rivers of the North. It signified nothing to these critics whether the tone, the spirit, or the style were caught from European writers or not. If a poet, in genuine Scott, or genuine Byron, compared his hero to a cougar or grisly bear—patriotically ignoring the Asiatic tiger or the African lion—the exclamation of the critic was, "How intensely American!" [7]

We submit that this is a false and narrow criterion, by which to judge of the true nationality of the author. Not in the subject, except to a partial extent, but in the management of the subject, in the tone and bearings of the thought, in the drapery, the colouring, and those thousand nameless touches, which are to be felt rather than expressed, are the characteristics of a writer to be sought. It is in these particulars that an author of original genius—no matter what his subject—will manifest his nationality. In fact, true originality will be always found identical with true nationality. A painter who should paint an American landscape exactly in the style of Salvator or of Claude, ought scarcely to be entitled an American painter. A poet who should write a hymn to Niagara in the blank verse of the Ulysses or the Princess, ought not to be entitled an American poet. In a word, he alone, who, in a style evolved from his own individual nature, speaks the thoughts and feelings of his own deep heart, can be a truly national genius. In the works of such a man, the character which speaks behind and through him— as character does not always speak in the case of men of mere talent, who in some respects are usually more or less under the sway of more commanding minds—will furnish the best and highest types of the intellectual character of his countrymen, and will illustrate most correctly, as well as most subtly—perhaps most correctly because most subtly—

the nature of the influences around him. In the poetry of such a man, if he be a poet, whether its scenes be laid in his native country or the land of faery, the pines of his own forests shall be heard to murmur, the music of his own rivers shall swell the diapason, the flowers of his own soil shall bud and burst, though touched perhaps with a more ethereal and lasting grace; and with a brighter and more spiritual lustre, or with a darker and holier beauty, it will be his own skies that look down upon the loveliest landscapes of his creation.

We regard the theory of Southernism in literature as a circumscription, both unnecessary and unreasonable, of the privileges of genius. Shakspeare was not less an Englishman when he wrote Antony and Cleopatra, than when he dramatized the history of the kings of England. Sir Walter was not less a Scotchman when he drew the characters of Louis XI. and Charles the Bold, than when he conceived the characters of Edie Ochiltree and Balfour of Burley. We do not suppose that until this theory germinated in the brain of its foolish originator, it ever occurred to an author that in his selection of subjects, he was to be bounded by certain geographical limits. And if in addition to the many difficulties which he has to overcome, the Southern author be expected, under the penalty of being pronounced un-Southern in tone, and unpatriotic in spirit, never to pass the Potomac on one side, or the Gulf on the other, we shall despair of ever seeing within our borders a literature of such depth and comprehensiveness as will ensure it the respect of other countries, or permanence in the remembrance of posterity. No! the domain of genius is as wide as the world, and as ancient as creation. Wherever the angel of its inspiration may lead, it has the right to follow—and whether exhibited by the light of tropic suns, or of the Arctic morning, whether embodied in the persons of ancient heroes, or of modern thinkers, the eternal verities which it aims to inculcate shall find in every situation, and under every guise, their suitable place, and their proper incarnation.

We should not like to convey the impression that we undervalue the materials for prose and poetry, which may be found in Southern scenery, Southern society, or Southern history. We are simply protesting against a narrow creed, by means of which much injustice may be done to a writer, who, though not less Southern in feeling than another who displays his Southernism on the surface of his books, yet insists upon the right to clothe according to the dictates of his own taste, and locate according to the dictates of his own thoughtful judgment, the creatures of his imagination. At the same time we are not blind to the spacious field which is opened to the Southern author within his own immediate country. The vast aboriginal forests which so weightily oppress us with a sense of antiquity, the mountains, tree-clad to the summit, enclosing unexplored Elysiums, the broad belt of lowland along the ocean, with its peculiar vegetation, the live-oak, stateliest of that stately family, hung with graceful tillandsia, the historical palmetto, and the rank magnificence of swamp and thicket, the blue aureole of the passion flower, the jessamine, with its yellow and fragrant flame, and all the wild luxuriance of a bountiful Flora, the golden carpet which the rice plant spreads for the feet of autumn, and the cotton field white as with a soft, warm snow of summer [8]—these are materials—and these are but a small part of them—from which a poet may draw an inspiration as genuine as that which touched with song the lips of English Thomson, or woke to subtler and profounder utterance the soul of English Wordsworth. Nor is the structure of our social life—so different from that of every other people, whether ancient or modern—incapable of being exhibited in a practical light. There are truths underlying the relations of master and slave; there are meanings beneath that union of the utmost freedom with a healthy conservatism, which, growing out of those relations, is characteristic of Southern thought, of which poetry may avail herself not only to vindicate our system to the eyes of the world, but to convey lessons which shall take root in the hearts of all mankind. We need not commend the poetical themes which are to be found in the history of the South; in the romance of her colonial period; in the sufferings and struggles of her revolution; in the pure patriotism of her warriors and statesmen, the sterling worth of her people, and the grace, the wit, the purity, the dignity, delicacy and self-devotion of her women. He who either in the character of poet or novelist shall associate his name with the South in one or all of the above-mentioned aspects, will have achieved a more enviable fame than any which has yet illustrated the literature of America.

We pass to a brief discussion of an error still more prevalent than the theory just dismissed. We know nothing more discouraging to an author, nothing which more clearly evinces the absence of any profound principles of criticism, than the light in which the labours of the poet and the novelist are very generally viewed at the South. The novel and the poem are almost universally characterized as light reading, and we may say are almost universally estimated as a very light and superficial sort of writing. We read novels and poems indeed, with some pleasure, but at the same time with the tacit conviction that we are engaged in a very trivial occupation; and we promise ourselves that, in order to make up for the precious moments thus thrown away, we shall hereafter redouble our diligence in the study of history or of mathematics. It is the common impression that while there is much practical utility in a knowledge of Euclid and the Calculus, no profit whatever is to be derived from works of poetry and fiction. Of two writers, one of whom should edit a treatise on the conic sections, and the other should give to the world a novel equal in tragic power and interest to the Bride of Lammermoor, the former would be considered the greater man by nine persons out of ten.

It would be from the purpose of this article to go into a minute examination of the prejudices upon which these opinions are founded. But we may be permitted a few words on the subject. What are the advantages which are supposed to result from the study of the mathematics—not, we mean, to those who are to devote their lives to science, but to that more numerous class who, immediately upon graduation, fling aside Playfair,[9] and separate into doctors, lawyers, and politicians? The answer is, we believe, that the study of mathematics is calculated to accustom the student to habits of close reasoning, and to increase his powers of concentration. Some vague generality is usually added about its influence in strengthening the mind.

Now, it is a notorious fact that mathematicians are for the most part bad reasoners out of their particular province. As soon as they get upon topics which do not admit of precise definitions and exact demonstrations, and which they, nevertheless, invariably insist upon subjecting to precise definitions and exact demonstrations, they fall naturally enough into all sorts of blunders and contradictions. They usually beg the question at the outset, and then by means of a most unexceptionable syllogism, they come to a conclusion which, though probably false in fact, is yet, it must be confessed, always logically consistent with their premises.

Now, it will not be denied that such a method of reasoning is the very worst possible which could be employed by a lawyer or a politician. The laws, and their various interpretations, the motives, the objects, the interest in their thousand contradictory aspects, which must form the staple of the arguments of professional and public men, are not to be treated like the squares and circles of geometry. Yet that a familiarity with mathematical modes of proof does not lead to the error of using those modes of proof upon subjects to which they are wholly inapplicable, is evident to anybody who has noticed the style of argument prevalent among the very young orators who have not long cut the apron strings which tied them to a too strictly mathematical Alma Mater. They bristle all over with syllogisms, write notes in the form of captions, invariably open a speech (that is if it be not a fourth of July oration, and if they have anything to prove) with a statement, and end with Q. E. D. corollary and scholium. Not until the last theories have been erased from their memory, or until they shall have learned by repeated reverses the absurdity of which they are guilty, do they begin to reason like men of practical sense.

It must not be inferred that we are arguing against the study of the mathematics. It has its uses—though we think not the uses commonly assigned to it. These we cannot stop to particularize, but we may mention that if it could do nothing but furnish us with the clearest idea we have of the nature of absolute truths, it would still be an important study.

We shall probably be thought paradoxical when we say that we believe that the study of poetry as an art in conjunction with the science of criticism—and this not with the design of writing poetry, but merely to enable the student to appreciate and to judge of it—will afford a better preparative training than all the mathematics in the world, to the legal or political debater. Poetry, as Coleridge well remarks, has a logic of its own; [10] and this logic being more complex, more subtle, and more uncertain than the logic of the demonstrative sciences, is far more akin than the latter can be to the dialectics of common life. And when we consider that while we are mastering this logic, we are at the same time familiarising ourselves with the deepest secrets of the human heart, imbuing our natures with the most refining influences, and storing our minds with the purest thoughts and the loveliest pictures of humanity, the utility of poetry as a study seems to be established beyond a question.

It seems strange, that in this nineteenth century, one should be called upon to vindicate poetry from aspersions which have been repeatedly and triumphantly disproved. Nevertheless, so generally accepted at the South is the prejudice which degrades poetry into a mere servant of our pleasures,[11] that upon most ears, truths, (elsewhere so familiar as to be trite) upon which it bases a loftier pretension, fall with the startling novelty of paradox. How many look upon the imaginative faculty simply as the manufacturer of pretty conceits; how few know it as the power which, by selecting and combining materials never before brought together, in fact, produces pictures and characters in which there shall be nothing untruthful or unnatural, and which shall yet be as new to us as a lately found island in the Pacific. How many of us regard poetry as a mere creature of the fancy; how few appreciate its philosophy, or understand that beneath all the splendour of its diction and imagery, there is in its highest manifestations at least a substratum of profound and valuable thought; how very few perceive the justice of the eloquent definition of Coleridge: "That poetry is the blossom and fragrance of all human wisdom, human passions, learning, and language;" [12] or are

prepared to see, as it is expressed in the noble verse of
Taylor, that

> Poetry is Reason's self-sublimed;
> Tis Reason's sovereignty, whereunto
> All properties of sense, all dues of wit,
> All fancies, images, perceptions, passions,
> All intellectual ordinance grown up
> From accident, necessity, or custom,
> Seen to be good, and after made authentic;
> All ordinance aforethought, that from science
> Doth prescience take, and from experience law;
> All lights and institutes of digested knowledge,
> Gifts and endowments of intelligence
> From sources living, from the dead bequests,—
> Subserve and minister.[13]

We hurry on to the comparative merits of history and
fiction.

It is not generally understood that a novel may be more
truthful than a history, in several particulars—but, perhaps,
most of all in the delineation of character. The historian,
hampered by facts which are not seldom contradictory, is
sometimes compelled to touch and retouch his portrait of
a character in order to suit those facts. Consequently, he
will often give us a character not as it existed, but his idea of
that character—a something, the like of which was never in
heaven above, nor on the earth beneath. On the other hand,
the novelist, whose only obligation is to be true to nature, at
least paints us possible men and women, about whose
actions we can reason almost with as much accuracy as if
they had really lived, loved, acted and died. In doing this, he
at once reaches a higher truth than is often attainable by
the historians, and imparts to us lessons far more profitable.
More of human nature can be learned from the novel of Tom
Jones than from a History of the whole Roman Empire—

written, at least, as histories are commonly written. Again, while it is to history we look for an account of the dynasties, the battles, sieges, revolutions, the triumphs and defeats of a nation, it is from the historical novel that we glean the best idea of that which it is infinitely more important for us to know—of the social state, the manners, morals, opinions, passions, prejudices, and habits of the people. We do not hesitate to say, that of two persons, one of whom has only read Hume's chapter on Richard I., and the other only the Ivanhoe of Scott, the latter will be by far the better acquainted with the real history of the period.

We need not say that we are not quite so silly as to believe that it is possible, by any force of argument, to bring about a reformation in the tastes of the reading community. It is, unfortunately, not in the power of a people to confer together and say, "Come, now, let us arise, and build up a literature." [14] We cannot call meetings, and pass resolutions to this purpose, as we do with respect to turnpikes, railways, and bridges. That genuine appreciation, by which alone literature is encouraged and fostered, is a plant of slow growth. Still, we think something may be done; but in the meanwhile let it not be forgotten that, in spite of every disadvantage, the South already possesses a literature which calls for its patronage and applause. The fate of that literature is a reproach to us. Of all our Southern writers, not one but Poe has received his due measure of fame. The immense resources and versatile powers of Simms are to this day grudgingly acknowledged, or contemptuously denied. There have been writers among us who, in another country, would have been complimented with repeated editions, whose names are now almost forgotten, and whose works it is now utterly impossible to obtain. While our centre-tables are littered with the feeble moralizings of Tupper, done up in very bright morocco; and while the corners of our newspapers are graced with the glibly versified common-places of Mackey, and of writers even more worthless than Mackey, there is, perhaps, scarcely a single bookseller in the United States, on whose face we should not encounter the grin of ignorance, if we chanced to inquire for the Froissart ballads of Philip Pendleton Cooke.

It is not without mortification that we compare the reception which the North gives to its literature to the stolid indifference of the South. There, at least, Genius wears the crown, and receives the tributes which are due to it. It is true, indeed, that not a few Northern authors have owed in part their successes to the art of puffing—an art nowhere carried to such a height of excellence as in the cities of New York and Boston. It is true that through the magic of this art, many a Bottom in literature has been decked with the flowers and fed with the apricots and dewberries of a short-lived reputation. But it is also true, that there is in the reading public of the North a well-founded faith in its capacity to judge for itself, a not inconsiderable knowledge of the present state of Poetry and Art, and a cordial disposition to recognize and reward the native authors who address it.

We are not going to recommend the introduction at the South of a system of puffing. "No quarter to the dunce," whether Southern or Northern, is the motto which should be adopted by every man who has at heart the interests of his country's literature. Not by exalting mediocrity, not by setting dullness on a throne, and putting a garland on the head of vanity, shall we help in the smallest degree the cause of Southern letters. A partiality so mistaken can only serve to depreciate excellence, discourage effort, and disgust the man of real ability. We have regretted to see the tenderness with which a volume of indifferent poetry is sometimes treated—for no other reason that we could discover than that it was the work of a Southerner—by those few clever and well-meaning critics, of whom the South is not altogether destitute. The effect of this ill-judged clemency is to induce those who are indisposed to admit the claims of Southern literature upon their admiration, to look with suspicion upon every verdict of Southern criticism.

We have but one course to suggest to those who are willing, from a painful conviction of the blended servility, superficiality, and antiquated bigotry of criticism among us, to assist in bringing about a reformation. It is to speak the rude truth always. It is to declare war equally against the slaves of English and Northern opinions, and against the slaves of the conventional schools of the eighteenth century. If argument fail, perhaps satire may prove a more effective weapon. Everything like old fogyism in literature should be remorselessly ridiculed. That pert license which consults only its own uneducated taste, and that docility which truckles to the *prestige* of a foreign reputation should be alike held up to contempt. It should be shown in plain, unflattering language that the unwillingness with which native genius is acknowledged, is a bitterer slander on the country and its intellect than any of the falsehoods which defile the pages of Trollope, Dickens, Marryatt, or Basil Hall.[15] It would be no injustice to tell those who refuse to credit that the South has done anything in prose or poetry, that in their own shallowness and stupidity they have found the best reasons for their incredulity; and they should be sternly reminded, that because a country annually gives birth to a thousand noodles, it does not follow that it may not now and then produce a man of genius. Nor should any hesitation be felt to inquire boldly into the manner in which the tastes of our youth are educated. Let it be asked on what principle we fill our chairs of belles-lettres; whether to discharge properly the duties of a critical teacher, a thorough acquaintance with English literature be not a rather indispensable requisite, and how it is that in one institution a learned professor shall maintain the Course of Time [16] to be the greatest of English epics, and in another an equally learned professor shall deny, on the ground that he could never read it, save as a very disagreeable task, the transcendent merits of Paradise Lost. Is it not a fact, of which we may feel not unreasonably ashamed, that a student may pass four years under these misleaders of youth, and yet remain ignorant of that most important revolution in imaginative literature—to us of the present day the most important of all literary revolutions—which took place a little more than half a century ago. The influence of the new spiritual philosophy in producing a change from a sensuous to a super-sensuous poetry, the vast difference between the school represented by Wordsworth, and the school represented by Pope, the introduction of that mystical element into our verse which distinguishes it from the verse of the age of Shakspeare, the theory of that analytical criticism which examines a work of art "from the heart outwards, not from surface inwards!" and which deduces its laws from nature and truth, not from the practice of particular writers; these surely are subjects which, in an institution devoted to the purpose of education, may not be overlooked without censure. At the risk of exciting the derisive smiles of those who attach more value to the settlement of a doubtful accent, or a disputed quantity, than to a just definition of the imaginative faculty, or a correct estimation of the scope and objects of poetry, we avow our belief that a systematic study of English literature, under the guidance of proper expounders—even at the expense of the curriculum in other respects—would be attended with the highest benefits to the student and the community. Such a course of study would assist more than anything else in bringing about that improvement in taste which we need so much, and for which we must look especially to the generation now growing up about us. We do not expect much from those whose opinions are already formed. It is next to impossible thoroughly to convert a confirmed papist; and there are no prejudices so difficult to overcome as the prejudices of pedantry and age.

After all, the chief impediment to a broad, deep, and liberal culture is her own self-complacency. With a strange inconsistency, the very persons who decry Southern literature are forever extolling Southern taste, Southern learning, and Southern civilization. There is scarcely a city of any size in the South which has not its clique of amateur critics, poets and philosophers, the regular business of whom is to demonstrate truisms, settle questions which nobody else would think of discussing, to confirm themselves in opinions which have been picked up from the rubbish of seventy years agone, and above all to persuade each other that together they constitute a society not much inferior to that in which figured Burke and Johnson, Goldsmith and Sir Joshua. All of these being oracles, they are unwilling to acknowledge the claims of a professional writer, lest in doing so they should disparage their own authority. It is time that their self-complacency should be disturbed. And we propose satire as the best weapon, because against vanity it is the only effective one. He who shall convince this, and every other class of critics to which we have alluded, that they are not in advance of their age, that they are even a little behind it, will have conferred an incalculable benefit upon them, and upon the South.

We shall not admit that in exposing the deficiencies of the Southern public, we have disparaged in the slightest degree the intellect of the South. Of that intellect in its natural capacity none can conceive more highly than ourself. It is impossible not to respect a people from whom have sprung so many noble warriors, orators and statesmen. And there is that in the constitution of the Southern mind, in the Saxon, Celtic and Teutonic elements of which it is composed, and in the peculiar influences amidst which these elements have been moulded together, a promise of that blending of the philosophic in thought with the enthusiastic in feeling, which makes a literary nation. Even now, while it is in one place trammeled by musty rules and canons, and in another left to its own unguided or misguided impulses, it would be unjust to deny it a quickness of perception, which, if rightly trained, would soon convert this essay into a slander and a falsehood. We will not believe that a people with such a mental character can remain much longer under the dominion of a contracted and illiberal culture. Indeed, we think the signs of a better taste may already be noticed. The circle of careless or prejudiced readers, though large, is a narrowing circle. The circle of thoughtful and earnest students, though a small one, is a widening circle. Young authors are rising up who have won for themselves at least a partial acknowledgment of merit. The time must come at last when the public shall feel that there are ideas characterizing Southern society, as distinguished from Northern and English society, which need the exposition of a new literature. There will be a stirring of the public mind, an expectation aroused which will ensure its own gratification, a demand for Southern prose and poetry, which shall call forth the poet and prose writer from the crowds that now conceal them, and a sympathy established between author and public, which shall infuse inspiration into the one, and heighten the pleasure and profit of the other. Then, indeed, we may look for a literature of which we shall all wear the honours. We shall walk over ground made classic by the imaginations of our poets, the thoughts we speak shall find illustration in verse which has been woven by Southern hearths; and the winds that blow from the land, and the waves that wash our level coast, shall bear to other nations the names of bards who know how to embody the spirit of their country without sinking that universality which shall commend their lessons to all mankind.

A Theory of Poetry[1]

IT IS not without some hesitation and considerable diffidence that I have selected Poetry as the subject of my essay. It is so familiar a topic, and to be familiar is in the opinion of so many to be commonplace, that I may well distrust my ability to give it interest. Yet after all it is not quite so old as the stars which the knowledge that they have shone for thousands of centuries has not made commonplace to those who look at them rightly. I encourage myself by the reflection that the freshness of my theme is not less eternal. Moreover as I design to discuss the subject with a special purpose, in regard to which I have some sincere and not carelessly digested opinions, I may hope perhaps to elicit so much attention at least as usually honest thought, however weakly embodied, and earnest convictions, however inadequately maintained, [receive].

I desire to arrive, if possible, at a comprehensive and satisfactory theory of poetry, but more especially to examine, and to enter my protest against certain narrow creeds which seem to me to be growing into fashion, to expose the falsity of that taste which is formed by particular schools, and which lead necessarily to a narrow and limited culture, and to assist, as far as it lies in my power, in the establishment of a generous and catholic criticism.

103

I must premise that in the first portion of my essay, I shall use the word poetry in accordance with common usage, as synonymous with poetical literature, or the embodiment of poetry in rhythmical language. As I proceed, however, I shall endeavour to show that it ought to [be] employed in a more restricted, and less material sense. I will add that in whatever illustrations I may use, I shall confine myself to English Poetry, as amply sufficient for my purpose.

There have been few poetical eras without their peculiar theories of poetry. But no age was ever so rich in poetical creeds as the first half of the present century. The expositions of some of these creeds are not without value, one or two indeed though incomplete are profound and philosophical; but the majority are utterly worthless. Every little poet "spins toiling out his own cocoon,"[2] and wrapping himself snugly in it to the exclusion of others, hopes to go down thus warmly protected to posterity.

I shall pass most of these theories to consider only two— one of which I shall discuss at some length. The first is that definition of poetry which represents it simply as the expression in verse of thought, sentiment, or passion; and which measures the difference between the poet and the versifier only by the difference between the depth, power, and vivacity of their several productions. This definition was ably advocated not long ago in a well-known Southern periodical, by one of the most acute of Southern writers.[3] It would not be difficult to prove its total inadequacy, but I do not think it necessary to do so, except so far as the proof of that inadequacy may be involved in the establishment of a theory altogether opposed to it. I am the less inclined to give it a minute examination, because though the idea is an old one, and in strict accordance with the common usage of the word poetry, it has never become popular, nor is it likely to become so, as it fails to satisfy even those who displeased they do not know why, and dimly conscious of the true faith, are yet unable to discover in their undefined emotions a logical refutation of the heresy. The genuine lovers of poetry feel that its essential characteristics underlie the various forms which it assumes, however dim and shadowy those characteristics may seem to them, and notwithstanding that they elude the search like the jar of gold which is fabled to be buried at the foot of the rainbow.

The second theory which I desire to examine critically was propounded a number of years ago.[4]

Poe begins his disquisition with the dogma that a long poem does not exist, that the phrase a long poem is simply a flat contradiction in "terms." He proceeds: "A poem deserves its title only inasmuch as it excites by elevating the soul. The value of a poem is in the ratio of this elevating excitement. But all excitements are, through a psychal necessity, transient. That degree of excitement which would entitle a poem to be so called at all, cannot be sustained throughout a composition of any great length. After the lapse of half an hour at the very utmost, it flags—fails—a revulsion ensues—and then the poem is in effect and in fact no longer such."

I am disposed to think that the young lady who pores till midnight over a metrical novel of Scott's, and wakes up the next morning with her bright eyes dimmed and a little swollen, or the young poet who follows for the first time the steps of Dante and his guide down to the spiral abysses of his imaginary hell, could not easily be induced to assent to the truth of these assertions. The declaration made with such cool metaphysical dogmatism that "all excitement[s] are through a psychal necessity, transient" needs considerable qualification. All violent excitements are indeed transient; but that moderate and chastened excitement which accompanies the perusal of the noblest poetry, of such poetry as is characterized not by a spasmodic vehemence and the short-lived power imparted by excessive passion, but by a thoughtful sublimity and the matured and almost inexhaustible strength of a healthy intellect, may be sustained, and is often sustained during a much longer period than the space of thirty minutes. I am willing to grant, however, that this excitement has also its limit, and that that limit is too narrow to permit the perusal, with any pleasure, at one sitting of more than a fraction of a poem of the length of Paradise Lost. I shall quote another paragraph, and then proceed to show that this acknowledgment leads to no deduction that justifies the theory which Poe has built upon it.

"There are, no doubt, many who have found difficulty in reconciling the critical dictum that the Paradise Lost is to be devoutly admired throughout with the absolute impossibility of maintaining for it, during perusal, the amount of enthusiasm which that critical dictum would demand. This great work, in fact, is to be regarded as poetical, only when, losing sight of that vital requisite in all works of art, Unity, we view it merely as a series of minor poems. If, to preserve its unity, we read it (as would be necessary) at a single sitting, the result is but a constant alternation of excitement and depression. After a passage of what we feel to be true poetry, there follows, inevitably, a passage of platitude which no critical prejudgment can force us to admire; but if, upon completing the work, we read it again, omitting the first book—that is to say commencing with the second —we shall be surprised at finding that admirable which we before condemned. It follows from all this that the ultimate, or absolute effect of even the best epic under the sun, is a nullity—and this is precisely the fact."

Let me call attention to the fact that even if the argument I have just read prove all it assumes to prove, it amounts only to this—it shows not that a long poem does not, or may not exist, but that if there could be such a thing as a long poem its effect except as a series of short poems would be null and void. This point, however it must be confessed, if properly established, would be an almost sufficient justification of Poe's theory; and I only mention it by way of causing it to be remarked that the demonstration is not quite so direct and positive as it appears at first sight, or as if the author had analyzed the work of which he speaks and shown at what point the first poem ends, and the second begins.

But I deny boldly and without reservation the truth of that assertion upon which the whole argument hinges, that to preserve in effect the unity of a great poem, it should be read through at a single sitting. And to substantiate my denial, I shall not fear to examine the effect of that very poem to which Poe has appealed.

I suppose then the Reader who takes up Paradise Lost to begin its perusal in a spirit not unbecoming that divine production, and with the reverence of one who enters upon holy ground. He must have "docile thoughts, and purgèd ears." [5] A poem the aim of which is "to justify the ways of God to man" is not to be entered upon at any season, and never when our only wish is to beguile a vacant moment. The time and even the place should be in harmony with the lofty theme. Charles Lamb in a spirit of proper appreciation says "that Milton almost needs a solemn service of music to be played" before we approach him. I can understand the earnest reader opening the book with feelings of devotion not much inferior to those which inspired the great bard himself in his sublime invocation to the third person of the Trinity.

> "And chiefly thou O Spirit that dost prefer
> Before all temples the upright heart and pure,
> Assist me for thou knowest! Thou from the first
> Wast present, and with mighty wings outspread,
> Dovelike, sat'st brooding o'er the vast abyss
> And mad'st it pregnant! What in me is dark
> Illumine, what is low, raise and support
> That to the height of this great argument,
> I may assert Eternal Providence
> And justify the ways of God to Man.

I affirm that he who takes up Paradise Lost in this spirit will lay it down at the completion of the first [book], or if (as is not unlikely) he should have been beguiled further, at the completion of the second book, not simply with an impression of satisfied[,] still less of satiated gratification, but in a state of mind in which awe and delight are blended together in a deep though sober rapture. I say too that upon his resuming the book at some future time, if he come to it with the same reverential precautions, and not as one who must finish a book to-night because he began it yesterday, there will occur no such utter disconnection between his perusal of the first, and his perusal of the second part of the poem as will produce an effect at all similar to that which is produced by the perusal of two distinct poems. I say that no hiatus of platitude, whether real or the result merely of jaded attention, is sufficient so to separate two parts of an artistically constructed poem like Paradise Lost, as to disturb the general harmony of its effect. And the thoughtful reader instead of sitting down to the study of the third book as to a new poem, brings with him all the impressions of his former reading to heighten the colour and deepen the effect of that which is before him. The continuation of the poem seems all the more beautiful because he is familiar with the beginning, and necessarily so from the roundness and completeness of a structure the parts of which add alike to the strength and grace of the whole and of each other. It has been correctly remarked of the extracts which go by the name of the beauties of Shakspeare,[6] that those passages lose more by being torn from the context than the dramas themselves would lose by being deprived of those passages altogether. This is true also, though doubtless not to so great an extent, of Paradise Lost, and it could not be true if each book, or part of a book, could affect us as strongly when considered as portions of a series of poems, as when regarded as fractions of an harmonious whole. For instance the situation of the happy pair in Paradise is rendered a thousand times more pathetic than it would have been otherwise by our knowledge of the power of the tempter who is plotting their destruction without; and of that power we could have no adequate conception if we had not seen the mighty Archdemon, his form not yet deprived of all its original brightness, his face intrenched with the deep scars of thunder, treading in unconquerable fortitude the surface of the burning marle, or if we had not beheld him in the mighty council assembled together under the roof of Pandemonium, assuming, in haughty preëminence of courage and hatred, the bold adventure of scouting with hostile purposes the universe of God Omnipotent, if we had not followed him in his dusky flight through Hell, and his encounter with the grim though Kingly Shadow, in his painful voyage through Chaos and his meeting, in which the mean but profound subtlety of his genius is brought distinctly into action, with the Archangel Uriel, and so on down to the moment when he alights upon the summit of Niphates and turns to reproach the Sun and blaspheme its Creator; if we had not from all these sources derived an indelible impression of the cunning, ferocity, the indomitable pride and daring recklessness of his character. Again, the fate of the guilty but repentant lovers touches us infinitely more deeply because we have been made familiar with the beauty of the home from which their sin has expelled them, that vast garden which with the eternal bloom of forests abound[s] with fruit more precious than that of the Hesperides, its undulations of hill and valley, its grottoes, fountains and "crisped brooks Rolling on orient pearl and sands of gold" [7] and feeding with nectar "Flowers of all hues, and without thorn the rose"—which with all this variety seems almost as extensive as a kingdom, and yet is compact enough to occupy only the champaign head of a steep and imperious wildness which surrounds it as with its protecting wall. But of course that which affects us most profoundly, and that which the Poet meant to affect us most profoundly, is not the loss of Eden, but the difference between the primal condition of innocence from which they fell, and which is described with a softness and purity that no merely amatory poet has ever equaled, with the state of mind in which after being dismissed by the angel, they look back to behold the Eastern Gate, "With dreadful faces thronged and fiery arms," and then turning, with the world before them, but with slow and wandering steps

"Through Eden take their solitary way."

I might go on and by minuter examination show still subtler connections between the several parts of the poem, but it is not necessary. I am satisfied to reaffirm my position that every portion of Paradise Lost is bound together by the closest relations, and helps to give force to all; and as the light about us is not produced solely by the direct rays of the Sun, but is composed of millions of atmospherical and other reflections, so the ultimate and aggregate effect of this truly great creation is made up of the innumerable lights and cross-lights which each book sheds upon the other[s]. So as day by day the reader, such a reader, at least, as I have described moves onward through the varied beauties and sublimities of the poem, its grand purport and harmonious proportions become more and more clearly apparent,—it is "vastness which grows, but grows to harmonize, All musical in its immensities—" [8] and when at the conclusion he lays the book reverently aside, it is with the feelings, not of one who has passed through a series of transient though noble excitements, but rather of one whose spirit filled with a long train of lofty thought and unsurpassable imagery, has grown almost to the size of that which it has been contemplating. To such a reader it would not seem too much to inscribe on the title-page of Paradise Lost, as an invitation to all those yet unacquainted with it, the fine stanza applied by a later Bard to the most magnificent of earthly temples

> "Enter! its grandeur overwhelms thee not;
>   And why? It is not lessened; but thy mind,
> Expanded by the genius of the spot,
>   Has grown colossal, and can only find
>   A fit abode wherein appear enshrined
> Thy hopes of immortality; and thou
>   Shalt one day, if found worthy, so defined,
> See thy God face to face, as thou dost now
> His Holy of Holies, nor be blasted by his brow." [9]

I shall not notice the sarcasms which Poe directs against those who measure the merit of a book by its length, as I have said nothing from which it could be inferred that I regard size as a criterion of excellence. It is one thing to say that a poem of twelve books may be good, and another thing to say that a poem is good because it contains twelve books. I am not going to deny, however, that a poem may be extended to so great a length as to preclude the possibility of its operating upon our feelings with unity of effect, as witness the Fairy Queen. Yet, it should be observed in justice to Spenser that *that* production is in fact, what Poe maintains the epic of Milton to be, a succession of poems having no real connection with each other. Perhaps the same may be said of the Iliad of Homer. I do not refer to the Columbiad [10] because if that ponderous production could be crushed into a space no bigger than that occupied by an epigram, not a drop of genuine poetry could be forced from it. If I should be asked to fix the limit beyond which a poem should not be extended, I can only answer that that must be left to the taste and judgment of the Poet based upon a careful and appreciative study of the few great masters. The ordeal of criticism will settle afterwards how far unity has been preserved or violated. In general it may be remarked that the plot of a poem should be so compact, as not to involve scenes and subjects of too great diversity. As a consequence of this principle, I have always regarded the Divine Comedy of Dante in its progress through Hell, Purgatory and Heaven as three distinct poems.

I do not wish it to be supposed that I look upon Paradise Lost as in all respects a perfect poem. It has many of the faults inseparable from all human productions. Indeed I so far agree with Poe that I concede that by no possibility can a poem as long as Paradise Lost be all poetry (Coleridge, the profoundest poetical critic of any age, says [it] ought not to be all poetry [11]) from beginning to end. However noble the theme, there will be parts and aspects which do not admit of the presence of genuine poetry. Herein, however, I differ from Poe, inasmuch as I maintain that these parts may be so raised above the ordinary level of prose by skillful verse as to preserve the general harmony of the poem, and not materially to injure its unity as a work of art. And in the distinction between poetry and a poem, between the spirit and its body which Poe recognizes when he comes to develope his theory, but which he blinks, or ignores altogether in his remarks upon Paradise Lost, I shall look for the justification of my position.

I hold that the confusion of these terms, of the subjective essence with the objective form[,] is the source of most of the errors and contradictions of opinion prevalent upon this subject. The two should be carefully distinguished, and should never, in any critical discussion, be allowed to mean the same thing. What then is Poetry? In the last century if you had asked this question, you would have been answered readily enough; and the answer would have been the definition which I dismissed a little while ago as unworthy of minute examination. But the deeper philosophical criticism of the present century will not remain satisfied with this surface view of poetry. Its aim is to penetrate to its essence, to analyze and comprehend those impressions and operations of the mind acting upon, and being acted upon by, mental or physical phenomena, which when incarnated in language, are recognized as the utterances of Poetry, and affect us like the music of angels. That this *is* the aim of present criticism I need not attempt to show by quotation, since it looks out on the pages of the most popular writers of the day. Indeed so very general has the feeling become that it is not of the forms of poetry that we need a description, that if you ask any man of common intelligence who is not merely a creature of facts and figures, to define poetry, he will endeavour to convey to you his idea, vague doubtless and shadowy[,] of that which in his imagination constitutes its spirit. The poets who attempt to solve the question look rather into themselves than into the poems which they have written. One, very characteristically, when his own poems are considered, defines it as "emotions recollected in tranquillity," and another as "the recollection of the best and happiest moments of the best and happiest minds."[12] These definitions—if definitions they can be called—are unsatisfactory enough, but they indicate correctly the direction in which the distinctive principle of poetry is to be sought.

I think that Poe in his eloquent description of the poetic sentiment as the sense of the beautiful, and in its loftiest action as a struggle to apprehend a supernal loveliness, a wild effort to reach a beauty above that which is about us, has certainly fixed with some definiteness one phase of its merely subjective manifestation.[13] It is indeed to the inspiration which lies in the ethereal, the remote, and the unknown, that the world owes some of its sweetest poems; and the poetry of words has never so strange a fascination as when it seems to suggest more than it utters, to call up by implication rather than by expression those thoughts which refuse to be embodied in language, and to hint at something ineffable and mysterious of which the mind can attain but partial glimpses. But in making this feeling, and this feeling only, constitute the poetic sentiment, Poe only verifies the remark of one of the most luminous critics of this century, that it is as little to men of peculiar and original genius as to the multitude, that we must look for broad and comprehensive critical theories. Such men have usu-

ally one faculty developed at the expense of others; and
the very clearness of their perception of one kind of excellence, impairs their perception of other and different kinds
of excellence. Their theories being drawn from their own
particular tastes and talents, just suffice to cover themselves
and those who resemble them. The theory of Poe leads
directly to the conclusion (and this he boldly avows) that
Tennyson is the noblest Poet that ever lived; since no other
poet that ever lived has possessed so much of that ethere-
ality and dim suggestiveness which Poe regards, if not as
the sole, at least as the highest characteristic of a poem. I
am constrained to add too that while the theory leads to
the conclusion that Tennyson is the noblest of poets, it
leads as surely to the conclusion that Poe is next to the
noblest. At the same time I must do Poe the justice to
acquit him of the petty vanity of wishing to lead his readers
to such a conclusion—his theory I regard as a natural and
logical result evolved from his own beautiful and very
peculiar genius. Like the fabled Narcissus, he fell in love
unconsciously with his own shadow in the water. I yield to
few, and only to that extravagant few who would put him
over the head of Milton himself, in my admiration of Poe;
and to *none* in a love which is almost a worship of Tennyson with whose poems I have been familiar from my boyhood, and whom I yet continue to study with ceaseless
profit and pleasure. But I can by no means consent to regard him as the first of Poets, and I am sure that Tennyson
himself would repudiate the compliment, and the theory
which seems to justify it. The very merit which that theory
mainly insists upon, is not characteristic of more than one
third part of the poems of Tennyson, who as a poet possesses
(what Poe had *not*) other qualities besides his intense spir-
itualism, of a more human and earthly tendency which

could not fail to bring him into affinity with other tastes, and constrain him to demand a broader creed.

In order to perceive the real narrowness of Poe's theory, it is but necessary to examine the list of those elements which he says induces in the poet the true poetical effect, and mark how carefully he selects only such appearances as are simply beautiful or simply mysterious, and how sedulously he excludes all that is sublime and terrible in the phenomena of nature. "The Poet," he says, "recognizes the ambrosia which nourishes his soul in the bright orbs of heaven,—in the volutes of the flower,—in the clustering of low shrubberies—in the slanting of tall Eastern trees—in the blue distance of mountains—in the grouping of clouds —in the gleaming of silver rivers—in the repose of sequestered lakes. He perceives [it] in the songs of birds—in the harp of Æolus—in the sighing of the night-wind—in the perfume of the violet—and in the suggestive odours that come to him at eventide over dim oceans from far distant and undiscovered lands." I have not enumerated all the influences to which he refers, but every one of them, will be found upon examination to bear the same general character of quiet and gentle beauty. Let me ask, in my turn, if there be no excitement of the poetical faculty in the clouded night as well as in the bright one,—in the rack of clouds by which the stars are driven in, as well as in the purple islands and crimson archipelagoes of sunset,—in the terror-stricken rain fleeing before the tempest, as well as in the gentle and refreshing showers of April—in the craggy dangers, as well as in the blue distance of mountains—in the rush of the tornado which opens a road through deep, untravelled and illimitable forests, as well as in the faint and fragrant sigh of the zephyr—in the lightening which shatters some great Admiral [14] doomed never again to be heard

of—in the ear-splitting crash of the thunder, the stricken
pine, and the blasted heath—in the tiger haunted jungles of
India—in the vast Sahara over which the sirocco sweeps
like the breath of hell—in the barren and lonely cape
strown with wrecks, and the precipitous promontory which
refuses to preserve even a single plank of the ships that
have been crushed against it—in the fearful tale suggested
by the discovery of a human skeleton upon a desert and
uninhabited island—in the march of the Pestilence—in the
bloody battle of freedom—and in the strange noises and
wild risks of an Arctic night when the Great Pack has
broken up, and an Arctic storm is grinding and hurling
the floes in thunder against each other.

In the same manner when the eloquent Poet comes to
seek the mental stimulants of poetry, he finds them "in all
unworldly motives—in all holy impulses—in all chivalrous
and self-sacrificing deeds"; but he does not, like the profounder Wordsworth, see them in the tranquil comforts of
home,—in the dignity of honest labour—in the charities
of the beggar—and in those every-day virtues over which
the human soul of Wordsworth's Muse broods in pleased
contemplation. He sees no appeal to the faculty in "the
common things that round us lie",—[15] in the fairy tales of
Science—in the magic of machinery—in the pen that writes
and the types that immortalize his argument—in truth as
truth merely—and in the lessons of which Nature is so
bountiful that they may be gathered from the very dust
that we tread beneath our feet.

I think that when we recall the many and varied sources
of Poetry, we must perforce confess that it is wholly impossible to reduce them all to the simple element of beauty.
Two other elements at least must be added: and these are
power when it is developed in some noble shape, and *truth*

—whether abstract or not—when it affects the common heart of mankind. For the suggestion of these two additional principles, I suppose I ought to say that I am indebted to Hunt; but I cannot help adding that I had fixed upon the same trinity of elements long before I became acquainted with his delightful book on Imagination and Fancy.[16]

It is then in the feelings awakened by certain moods of the mind when we stand in the presence of Truth, Power, and Beauty, that I recognize what we all agree to call Poetry. To analyze the nature of these feelings, inextricably tangled as they are with the different faculties of the mind, and especially with that great faculty which is the prime minister of Poetry,—Imagination—is not absolutely necessary to the present purpose. Let us be satisfied with having ascertained the elements which excite in us the sentiment of Poetry, and, with having thus in a measure fixed its boundaries; and proceed at once to consider it as it appears when embodied in language.

Of course I hold with those who maintain that Poetry may develope itself in various modes—in Painting, Sculpture, Architecture, Music, as well as in words. Indeed there is no divining in what quarter this subtle and ethereal spirit may *not* make its appearance. Though verse is its most natural garment, it sometimes looks out upon mankind in the guise of prose where "its delights Are dolphin-like, and show themselves above The element they sport in." [17] We are talking with a lovely, intelligent woman who assures us that she has no expression for the Poetry that is in her, and afterwards proceeds to recount [the] story of some noble martyrdom, when behold! in the proud flush that mantles her forehead, and the smile that comes up from the depth of her beautiful eyes, the visible presence of Poetry itself.

Our present business, however, is only with the development of Poetry in words.

I look upon every poem as strictly a work of art, and on the Poet, in the act of putting poetry into verse, simply as an artist. If the Poet have his hour of inspiration (though I am so sick of the cant of which this word has been the fruitful source, that I dislike to use it) it is not during the work of composition. A distinction must be made between the moment when the great thought strikes for the first time along the brain, and flushes the cheek with the sudden revelation of beauty, or grandeur,—and the hour of patient and elaborate execution. The soul of the Poet, though constrained to utter itself at some time or other, does not burst into song as readily as a maiden of sixteen bursts into musical laughter. Many poets have written of grief, but no poet with the first agony at his heart, ever sat down to strain that grief through iambics.[18] Many poets have given expression to the first raptures of successful love, but no poet, in the delirium of the joy, has ever babbled it in anapests. Could this have been possible, the poet would be the most wonderful of improvisers, and perhaps a poem would be no better than what improvisations always are.

It would be easy to prove the truth of these remarks by the confessions of the Poets themselves. Poe has described to the world the manner in which he slowly built up the poem of the Raven.[19] A greater poet than Poe speaks of himself as "not used to make A present joy the matter of his song," [20] and of his poems, which the "Muse accepts, *deliberately* pleased," [21] as "*thoughtfully* fitted to the Orphean lyre." The labour through which Tennyson has attained that perfection of style which is characteristic of his poems, must have been almost infinite. And Matthew Arnold—a poet not widely known in this country, but one who in the estimation of the English critical Public—sits not very far below Tennyson—separates as I have separated the hour of insight, from the hour of labour.

> "We cannot kindle when we will
>   The fire that in the heart resides;
> The spirit bloweth and is still;
>   In mystery our soul abides;
> *But tasks in hours of insight willed*
> *May be through hours of gloom fulfilled.*" [22]

Does this fact lessen the merit of the Poet, or the charm of his poem? I do not see why it should do so, any more than the fact that the Eve in your library which was once but a beautiful idea in the mind of its creator, was slowly chiseled from a block of shapeless marble, should deprive the sculptor of his glory, or mar for a single instant the effect of the faultless symmetry and suggestive countenance of the statue.

It must not be forgotten that my present aim is to show how it is possible that a poem, without being all poetry from beginning to end, may be complete as a work of art. Now there are two classes of poets differing essentially in their several characters. The one class desires only to utter musically its own peculiar feelings, thoughts, sentiments, or passion, without regard to their truth, or falsehood, their morality or their want of morality, but in simple reference to their poetical effect. The other class with more poetry at its command than the first, regards Poetry simply as the minister—the highest minister indeed but still only the minister—of Truth, and refuses to address itself to the sense of the Beautiful alone. The former class is content only to create Beauty, and writes such poems as the Raven of Poe,

or the Corsair of Byron. The latter class aims to create
Beauty also, but it desires at the same time to mould this
Beauty into the shape of a temple dedicated to Truth. It is
to this class we owe the authorship of such poems as the
Paradise Lost of Milton, the lines on Tintern Abbey, and
the Excursion of Wordsworth, and the In Memoriam of
Tennyson. The former class can afford to write brief and
faultless poems because its end is a narrow one; the latter
class is forced to demand an ampler field, because it is influenced by a vaster purpose.

Take a poet of the last mentioned class at the commence-
ment of his work. Imbued with a love of truth, conscious of
the noble character of his mission as a poet, convinced
that a poem should, to use the words of Bacon, help and
confer to magnanimity, morality as well as delectation,[23]
he chooses a subject the beauty of which may be so developed as to subserve an ulterior and loftier end. The end of
Milton's poem is the glory of God and a justification of his
ways toward man. The end of the poems of Wordsworth
is to evolve the spiritual meanings that lie behind the
phenomena of Nature, and to show that the materials of
Poetry may be gathered from the common and familiar
things of existence. The end of the poems of Tennyson who,
in his large Nature touches Poe upon the one side, and
Wordsworth on the other, is at times, as purely the creation
of beauty as Poe could desire it to be. But it is not less
often to inculcate the profoundest lessons of a human philosophy, and to do this he sounds in one poem the remotest
metaphysical depths, he embodies the whole history of a
sorrow in another, and in a third he converts into magnificent verse, the doubts, fears and perplexities through which
the soul attains at last a ground on which to rest its hopes
of immortality.

The poet who has such ends as these in view is not likely to measure the length of his poem by the rules of Poe's theory. If his subject be in the main poetical, he is careless if its complete development, involve the treatment of here and there a prosaic topic, and necessitate the composition of a few thousand instead of one hundred and fourteen lines. But at the same time in the development of this subject, he will not forget that he is an artist; and that he is bound to produce, as far as possible, an harmonious work of art. He will take care that all his topics have reference to the general purpose of his poem; and when they are unpoetical, he may not seldom use them as the musician uses his discords, or as the painter his shadows, to strengthen by contrast the effect of that which is genuinely poetical. He will endeavour also, by every artifice of verse and language, to raise these necessarily unpoetical portions, as near as may be, to the height of the loftier portions of his creation. Thus Milton has contrived, by a melodious arrangement, to impart a wonderful charm to a mere list of geographical names. And thus Tennyson by clearness and sometimes picturesqueness of expression, and by the unequalled perfection of his rhythm, has succeeded in giving a poetical air to thoughts which in any other hands would have been the baldest and most prosaic abstractions.

It seems to me that I have now made plain what I mean when I say that a poem may be complete without being, in the highest and most legitimate sense, poetical in all its parts. If a poem have one purpose, and the materials of which it is composed be so selected and arranged as to help enforce it, we have no right to regard it as a series of minor poems because there may occur an occasional flaw in the structure. And he who persists in reading such a poem as so many short ones, besides losing the pleasure of contemplating the symmetrical development of a work [of] art, will fail to grasp the central purpose of the Poet.

It seems to me that I may strengthen still farther my theory that truth as much as beauty is a source of poetry, by a reference to the works of a Poet who always refused to separate them. When Poe speaks of the impossibility of "reconciling the obstinate oils and waters of Poetry and Truth," he is, unconsciously to himself, confounding Truth with Science and Matter of fact. It is of course impossible to see poetry in the details of business, in the arguments and commonplaces of politicians, or in the fact that the three angles of any triangle are equal to two right angles. But there *is* poetry in the truths of the mind and heart, in the truths that affect us in our daily relations as men, and even in the grand, general truths of Science, when they become familiar to us, and help us to understand and appreciate the beauty of the Universe. This is what Coleridge meant in part when he represents Poetry as "the blossom and the fragrance of all human knowledge, human thoughts, human passions, emotions, language," [24] and what Wordsworth meant when he not less eloquently describes it "as the breath and finer spirit of all knowledge; the impassioned expression which is in the countenance of all Science." [25] But a few specimens from those poems, the source of whose inspiration is truth, will do more than any remarks of mine to establish my opinion.

The poet who first taught the few simple, but grand and impressive truths which have blossomed into the poetic harvest of the 19th century, was Wordsworth. The poetic literature of the age which preceded the appearance of Wordsworth was in general wholly artificial and conventional. In saying this, I do not mean to condemn it—on the contrary, I am grateful to those poets who gave expression to the very little poetry which was to be found in the forms, fashions, and sentiments of an age which, in the face of the materialism about us, I believe to have been infinitely more material than the present one. But the moment these poets wandered away from society to enter the domain of Nature, they became blind, or if they saw at all, it was through a haze of falsehood. The descriptive poems of Pope are below contempt. I need not remind you of the famous moonlight scene in the Iliad which Coleridge, De Quincey and Macaulay have shown to be full of the most absurd inaccuracies. Passages equally inaccurate might be taken from Windsor Forest. It was to Wordsworth, mainly, that we owe that couching of the Poetic eye which enables it to observe truly the appearances of Nature, and to describe them correctly.

I have already said something as to the aims of the poems of Wordsworth. When he began to write, it was with the purpose of embodying in all the poetic forms at his command, the two truths of which the poets and readers of the time seemed to him completely incognizant. These were, first, that the material and stimulants of poetry might be found in some of the commonest things about us, and second that behind the sights, sounds and hues of external Nature, there is "something more than meets the senses, something undefined and unutterable which must be felt and perceived by the soul" [26] in its moments of rapt contemplation. It is this latter feeling that constitutes the originality of Wordsworth. It is not to be found in Shakspeare or his contemporaries. It is not to be found in Milton, and of course not in Milton's successors, not in Dryden or Pope, not in Thomson or Cowper. It appeared for the first time

in literature, in the lines of Wordsworth written near Tintern Abbey. Since then it has been caught up and shadowed
forth in every shape by every poet from Byron to the present English Laureate.[27] I cannot understand how anyone
can read that profound poem, and remain satisfied with
the dictum of Poe that the sole office of a poem should be
the development of beauty alone. I shall not apologize for
quoting an extract from it. After describing the mere ani-
mal pleasure with which the appearances of Nature affected
his youth, the poet proceeds to speak of those moods in
which he has looked behind those appearances to detect
the spirit of which they were but the varied expression.

> "I cannot paint
> What then I was. The sounding cataract
> Haunted me like a passion; the tall rock
> The mountain, and the deep and gloomy wood
> Their colours, and their forms, were then to me
> An appetite; a feeling and a love
> That had no need of a remoter charm,
> By thought supplied, or any interest
> Unborrowed from the eye. That time is past,
> And all its aching joys, are now no more,
> And all its dizzy raptures. Not for this
> Faint I, nor mourn, nor murmur; other gifts
> Have followed, for such loss I would believe
> Abundant recompense. For I have learned
> To look on Nature not as in the hour
> Of thoughtless youth; but hearing oftentimes
> The still, sad music of humanity,
> Nor harsh, nor grating, though of ample power
> To chasten and subdue. And I have felt
> A presence that disturbs me with the joy
> Of elevated thoughts; a sense sublime
> Of something far more deeply interfused
> Whose dwelling is the light of setting suns

And the round ocean, and the living air,
And the blue sky, and in the mind of man
A motion and a spirit, that impels
All thinking things, all objects of all thought,
And rolls through all things."

It is in the prefatory verses to the Excursion, that he announces his doctrine that the domain of Poetry lies as well in the familiar as in the remote,

"Beauty—a living presence of the earth
Surpassing the most fair ideal forms
Which craft of delicate spirits hath composed
From earth's materials—waits upon my steps;
Pitches her tents before me as I move,
An hourly neighbour. Paradise and groves,
Elysian, fortunate fields, like those of old
Sought in the Atlantic main, why should they be
A history only of departed things,
Or a mere fiction of what never was?
For the discerning intellect of man
When wedded to this goodly universe
In love and holy passion, shall find these
A simple produce of the common day." [28]

Wordsworth indeed always regarded the poet as a teacher and in the elucidation in various modes of the ideas conveyed in the passages which I have quoted, he recognized the business of his life. And in sooth if he had done nothing more than give these truths to the world, he would be entitled to our lasting gratitude. In his many exemplifications of them in his poems, he has opened new and unexplored regions of loveliness, he has shown us how it is possible by the mere act of pressing a spade into the earth, to bring it up rich in poetical ore; and he has taught us how the soul may detect, not only in the changing clouds and the succession of the flowers, but in the fixed and steady lineaments of rock and mountain, [an] expression ever varying; and as if he had given us another sense, though in reality he has only roused us to the knowledge of one which we must often have used unconsciously, but whose revelations we had, in our ignorance, interpreted wrongly he has enabled us to see even in the material universe about us, the actual presence of the power of the Invisible.

But it is not the revelation alone of the two cardinal doctrines of his poetic creed that we owe to Wordsworth. We are indebted to him for the inculcation of a love of nature which, to the passionate extent it was carried by Wordsworth, had never before found expression in the literature of any age or people. We are indebted to him for hundreds of single lines, which in their brief compass enshrine more beauty and wisdom than is to be found in many poems, and which have stamped themselves like proverbs on the common memory. In the two books of the Excursion entitled A Churchyard among the Mountains, and which following out my theory, I have always separated in my mind from the body of the work, as composing a complete poem in themselves, he has described with exquisite pathos, the heart-histories of the humble; and in the Prelude—

> An Orphic song indeed
> A song divine of high and passionate thoughts,
> To their own music chanted" [20]

he has given us with as much metaphysical truth, as poetic power, an account of the gradual growth and formation of a poetic mind, while in the ode on the Intimations of Immortality from Recollections of early Childhood, which, if we except perhaps Milton's Hymn of the Nativity, is undoubtedly the noblest ode in the language, he has flung a new and sacred lustre over the life of Infancy.

In this brief summary, I have by no means gone over all the ground upon which Wordsworth has built the immortal structure of his fame. I have said enough, however, to show how profoundly he recognized the inspiration of Truth. But I cannot help calling the attention further to the manner in which the element of truth appears in his descriptions of the feminine character. No other poet save Tennyson, and the great bard who imagined Cordelia and Miranda, Ophelia and Imogen, has ever depicted that character with the purity, tenderness and fidelity of Wordsworth. There are no amatory poems in Wordsworth—none at least of that sort which Moore and Byron have made popular, in which a woman is in the same breath addressed as an angel, and wooed as the frailest of sinners. It is usually only in her relations of wife, mother, sister or friend that Wordsworth alludes to woman; and he speaks of her always with the respect, and at the same time, with the gentle and courteous freedom of an affectionate and honourable husband, or brother. Familiar as they probably are to all present, I cannot resist the temptation of quoting the lines in which the interesting wife of the poet will go down to posterity

> "She was a phantom of delight
> When first she gleamed upon my sight;
> A lovely Apparition, sent
> To be a moment's ornament;
> Her eyes as stars of twilight fair,
> Like twilight's too her dusky hair;
> But all things else about her drawn
> From May-time and the cheerful dawn,
> A dancing Shape, an Image gay,
> To haunt, to startle and waylay.

I saw her upon nearer view
A spirit yet a woman too!
Her household motions light and free
And steps of virgin liberty;
A countenance in which did meet
Sweet records, promises as sweet;
A creature not too bright and good
For human nature's daily food;
For transient sorrows, simple wiles,
Praise, blame, love, kisses, tears, and smiles.

And now I see with eye serene
The very pulse of the machine;
A Being breathing thoughtful breath,
A traveller between life and death;
The reason firm, the temperate will,
Endurance, foresight, strength, and skill;
A perfect woman nobly planned
To warn, to comfort, and command;
And yet a spirit still, and bright
With something of an angel light." [30]

Wordsworth never could have been brought to agree
with Poe that a true poem is written for the poem's sake
alone. The theory which Poe very naturally evolved from
his own genius, Wordsworth quite as naturally would have
thought incompatible with the high office of a poet as
thinker, seer, teacher, and bard. On the other hand, the
broader vision of Tennyson has enabled him to detect the
truth which lies upon the side of Poe, and the truth which
lies upon the side of Wordsworth. The proof that a poet
may aim at beauty alone without respect to an ulterior
purpose, he sees in every daisy and buttercup of an English
meadow.

> "O, to what uses shall we put
> The wild-weed flower that simply blows?
> And is there any moral shut
> Within the bosom of the rose?" [31]

But not the less does he recognize the right of the poet to make his art the vehicle of great moral and philosophical lessons, not less does he recognize his right to grapple with the darkest problems of man's destiny, to discuss the fears and perplexities of the spirit, and the faith which triumphs over them, and even to drop now and then, a silken line into the dim sea of metaphysics.

I have been induced to undertake a refutation of Poe's theory while attempting to establish another which (such is the difficulty of the subject) may not improbably turn out to be equally objectionable, not because I believe it to be the one most prevalently adopted, but because I regard it as the one most artfully put, and at the same time most likely to excite interest in a Southern audience. I have not time to examine any other of those theories which seem to me to present false views of poetry. There is an admirably written essay prefixed to the second edition of the poems of Matthew Arnold in which that poet endeavours to show that all the poets of the present century have been working on mistaken principles, and that the ancients were the only true masters of the poetical art. A theory (to the full as true as Poe's) might also be drawn from the works of the Brownings which would lead to the exclusion of Poe from the roll of great poets, as surely as the theory of Poe would lead to the exclusion of the Brownings. I do not regret, however, the necessity of passing over the many plausible half-truths which go to make up the creed of this or that poet, as the principal object I have proposed to myself in this essay, is to call attention to the narrowness of them all. A very little examination will generally prove that they have grown out of the idiosyncrasies of the poets themselves, and so necessarily seldom attain a greater breadth

than suffices to shelter the theorist and the models from
which he has drawn his arguments and his inspiration. Yet
every one of these creeds has its disciples; and the consequence is, the growth of particular schools in the study
of which the taste becomes limited, and the poetic vision,
except in one direction, is deprived of all its clearness. I
am not protesting against an evil existing only in my imagination. I have known more than one young lover of poetry
who read nothing but Browning, and there are hundreds
who have drowned all the poets of the past and present in
the deep music of Tennyson. But is it not possible with the
whole wealth of English literature at our command to attain views broad enough to enable us to do justice to genius
of every class and character[?] That certainly can be no
true poetical creed which leads directly to the neglect of
those masterpieces which though wrought hundreds or
thousands of years ago, still preserve the freshness of their
perennial youth. It is not from gratitude simply—though
we owe them much—to the many poets whose "thoughts
have made rich the blood of the world" [32] that I desire to
press their claims upon attention. In the possession of a
fame as immortal as Truth and Nature, they can afford to
look with indifference upon a temporary suspension of
admiration. The injury falls only on such as slight them,
and the penalty they pay, is a contracted and contracting
insight, the shutting on them forever of many glorious vistas
into the universe of mind and matter, and the loss of
thousands of images of grace and beauty and grandeur.
Oh! rest assured that there are no stereotyped forms of
poetry. It is a vital power, and may assume any guise, and
take any shape—at one time towering like an Alp in the
darkness, and at another sunning itself in the bell of a tulip,

or the cup of a lily. Until you shall have learned to recognize it in all its various developments, you will have no right to echo back the benison of Wordsworth,

> "Blessings be on them and eternal praise,
> The poets who on earth have made us heirs
> Of *Truth* and *pure delight* in heavenly lays!" [33]

Appendix

WILLIAM J. GRAYSON

What is Poetry?[1]

〜〜〜〜〜〜〜〜〜〜〜〜〜〜〜〜〜〜〜〜〜〜〜〜〜〜〜〜〜

What is Poetry? What constitutes the poetic Character?
What are the distinctive features of the School of English
   Poets?

THESE inquiries are short, but they cover a large space. We
will confine our present article to the first—to the question,
what is Poetry?

Can any question be more common-place? To ask what
is prose would hardly be more so. Who is unable to answer
either the one or the other? In the multitude of books, what
reader is at a loss to determine which one is poetry and
which prose? Yet, if we judge from the number and vague-
ness of the descriptions of poetry which we frequently hear,
we must conclude that it is the most difficult of all things
to understand or define. It is a mysterious power. Everybody admires it, but nobody condescends to tell what it is.
Poet and philosopher, orator and critic, have all in turn
exalted it with equal zeal, if not equal knowledge, and have
so clothed it in robes of purple and fine linen, as to induce
us to regard it as something supernatural and divine.

It is natural enough that the Poet should magnify his
calling. His craft in his eyes is something more than human.
It gives to airy nothings local habitations and names. It is
the gift of a celestial power. The Muse speaks through the

135

Poet and inspires his song. He never opens his lips without supplicating her aid. Homer invokes her to sing the wrath of his hero and its dire evils to the Grecian host. Virgil supplicates all the divinities of earth and heaven to help him while he instructs the husbandman in the science of sowing and reaping, of planting the vine and olive, of managing bees and cattle. Milton asks the Heavenly Muse's aid when he essays things unattempted yet in *prose or rhyme*. It is a divinity always that sings, the poet is the instrument only. He himself has about him something that is divine. No vulgar joys or employments command attention with him on whom, at his birth, Melpomene has looked with favoring eyes. He is prophet as well as poet—*sacer vates*. He belongs to the sanctuary. Let the multitude—the *profanum vulgus*— stand apart and afar. His communings are with Gods or Celestial Spirits. He is borne aloft by no earthly wing—*non usitata penna*—and his head is among the stars.

We submit ourselves to these voices of the oracle and our minds are filled with vast and vague conceptions of the character of the Poet and the nature of his art. Now and then an infidel is rude enough, perhaps, to question their divinity. Occasionally a barbarian may be found savage as Coleridge's Schoolmaster, old Bowyer,[2] when animadverting on the performances of his young bards whose verses were filled with Lyres, Pierian Springs and inspiring Muses.— "Lyre, harp!" he would say; poh, boy, you mean pen and ink; "Pierian Spring!" ah, true, the pump in the Cloister yard; "the Muse!"—yes, yes, I understand, you are thinking of your nurse's daughter. But such carping spirits are outside barbarians and evidently come within the meaning and limits of Horace's "*odi profanum vulgus et arceo*."[3] Those of gentler training hold a better faith and cherish devout and indefinite conceptions of the artist and the sacred art—

"the vision and the faculty divine." It is their attention that the Poet invokes in his *"favete linguis,"* and not that of the incredulous and profane.

But if the Poet glorifies his calling, the Orator is hardly behind him in doing it reverence. In the exuberance of his rhetoric he forgets or scorns all the requisitions of logic or sober thought. How the Roman orator expatiates on the divine arts, in his defence of the poet Archias! [4] "Other arts, he tells us, are dependent on learning, practice, persevering efforts, but the Poet derives his power from nature alone; he is self-dependent; there breathes through his soul a certain divine spirit, the peculiar gifts of the Gods." Hence, he says, our Ennius, the old Roman bard, called the Poets sacred. Among the most refined and cultivated nations, their name is hallowed. No people is so barbarous as not to reverence it. Rocks and deserts echo the Poet's song. Cruel wild beasts stand still arrested by the charms of his voice. Cities and States contend for the honor of being his birth place. What are the glorious exploits of the hero if he fails to obtain the aid of the sacred bard, who alone can give them immortality[?] The wonderful deeds of his own consulship, the wisdom, the eloquence, the statesmanship, which saved the great republic and crushed the conspiracy of Catiline, would have been incomplete, and without their crowning glory in his eyes, had the Muse's votary, whose cause he was defending, withheld the expected eulogy.

Grave Philosophers take up the subject with almost equal enthusiasm. If Plato banished the Poets from his ideal republic, it was, perhaps, an indirect compliment to the seductive powers of their art which overshadowed the Philosopher's less alluring dreams and visions. But one at least equal to Plato, does all honor to the gentle craft. No more noble sketch of the limits and purposes of poetry can be conceived than that which Bacon gives in the "Advancement of Learning," nor is there one that more severely rebukes the low and vile purposes to which the art of poetry has been sometimes degraded by its unworthy votaries. He makes it to be [the] office of Poetry to repair the inequalities of fortune, to redress the wrongs of virtue, to introduce us into a higher world of being, to cheer, purify and elevate the heart.

The Poets, Orators, and Philosophers may exalt the divine art extravagantly, but they are honest as well as earnest in their praise. Their commendations do no harm if they are received with a discreet and proper spirit. We are not able to say as much for the Critics. Their zeal is not always attendant on knowledge. They love refinements and subtle speculations. They are not content with seeing through a millstone no better or farther than other people. They make poetry not divine only, but unintelligible. They embody the eulogies of rhetorician and poet in canons and definitions. In discussing the nature of poetry, they do what Selden [5] says the Catholic does in the question of transubstantiation —they turn rhetoric into logic, not without evil consequences. Poetry becomes transmuted, in their hands, into an indefinable something, which is neither prose nor verse, but which may be found indifferently in either. Poets and Orators exalt poetry vaguely by extravagant figures of speech. The Critics turn these figures into curious distinctions and definitions, until at last we are puzzled to know where poetry or prose begins or ends.—Poetry becomes prose and prose becomes poetry. The confusion of ideas and language is endless, and we talk of prose poems and poetic prose, as if these terms were not as incongruous as the phrases, round square and oblong circle.

These vague conceptions naturally lead to false theories.

They are numerous accordingly. One Critic announces, authoritatively, what he calls the invariable principles of poetry, and according to these, gives judgment on all poems and poets. Another decides that it is identical with the delineation of the forms of external nature or of passion and emotion, subjects it to the terms of a corresponding definition, and thus limits the art to one only of its numerous departments. So Aristotle, if one may venture to introduce so great a name, defines poetry to be an imitative art. He had in his mind, probably, that province of poetry which exhibits to the eye, on the stage, a mimic representation of the actions and passions of mankind, and which makes so large a part of the glory of Athenian literature. To this alone the definition seems properly applicable. So every Critic has his bed of justice in the shape of theory or canon, and poetry is cramped or curtailed to suit its length, breadth and depth.

Nothing is more amusing, in their way, than these fanciful standards of criticism, and nothing more ridiculous than the conclusions to which they sometimes lead. One Critic, in conformity with his essential principles of poetry, determines that certain classes of poets are no poets at all. They are not conversant with that order of subjects to which, by his essential principles, all poetry is confined. He excludes the Satirists, for example, from the precincts of Parnassus. The satires of Juvenal, Horace, Dryden, Churchill, are not poems. Mr. Harnay [6] thinks that the very existence of the doubt as to their claims shows the accuracy of the theory by which they are excluded. His inference ought to be that the absurdity of the conclusion proves the falsity of the theory. The doubt exists no where except in the minds of those who maintain the opinion that produces it.

Poets, termed critics, like Bowles [7] and Wordsworth, are

as prone as others to false speculation and erroneous judgments. Wordsworth began his career with a creed of essential principles. In those days he disparaged Virgil, thought slightingly of Gray's elegy, repudiated Pope, and could see nothing admirable in Johnson's magnificent imitations of Juvenal. He lived to renounce his theory, at least in practice. Indeed, he freely confessed, when older and wiser, that he once talked a great deal of what he was willing his friends should entirely forget. Yet he was tenacious of his creed. He did not often praise the works of other poets. He was unlike Walter Scott in that respect. He was also unlike him in being always ready to defend his own. In one of these defences, contained in a letter to an American friend, who had ventured to *hesitate dislike* to the simple beauties of the "Idiot Boy," he replies to the criticism in these words: "You begin what you say upon the 'Idiot Boy,' with the observation that nothing is a fit subject for poetry which does not please. But here follows a question: Does not please whom? Some have little knowledge of natural imagery of any kind and, of course, little relish for it; some are disgusted by the very mention of the words pastoral poetry, sheep or shepherds; some cannot tolerate a poem with a ghost or any supernatural agency in it. * * * * Others are disgusted with the naked language of some of the most interesting passions of men because it is indelicate or gross or vulgar, as many fine ladies could not bear expressions in the 'Mother' and the 'Thorn,' and as in the instance of Adam Smith, who could not endure the ballad of 'Clym of the Clough,' because the author had not written like a gentleman. * * * * I return then to the question, please whom or what? I answer, human nature, as it has been and will be. And where are we to find the best measure of this? I answer, from within." [8]

All this is very true, and it is precisely because it is true that we see so great a variety in the poetry of all nations. Because tastes are different, therefore poetry assumes a diversity of forms, applies itself to all subjects, addresses itself to all minds, and becomes, like them, multiform in shape and character. The resources of the poets for pleasing must be as various as the tastes to be pleased. If there are "Idiot Boys" there must be "Londons," and "Rapes of the Lock," and "Elegies in Country Church Yards." If we have Wordsworths, we must have Virgils and Popes also. The diversity in taste growing out of the difference, mental and moral, of human minds, is natural and unavoidable. It is this variety that is alone consonant to what Wordsworth calls the "eternal nature and great moving spirit of things." [9] Each class of readers has its favorite subjects and poets, and admires and prefers them with equal reason.

These varieties in taste and judgment meet us at every turn. There is hardly a poem in the English language, or we suppose in any other, which is not differently valued by different classes of readers. Ossian was once almost universally admired. Blair gives it a high place among poems. The great Napoleon was addicted to reading it. Dr. Johnson, on the other hand, treated scornfully the ghostly creations of the Northern bard, and the same diversity of appreciation still exists, with, perhaps, a diminished number in the ranks of his admirers.

The old dramatic writers have been at one time neglected, at another eulogized without limit.

The ancient ballad poetry, once almost forgotten, has again taken possession of the public mind. The ruder and more uncouth the language and the metre, the greater the admiration. Chevy Chace modernized as criticized by Addison, was not judged to be equal to the old rough original. [10]

Everybody read, everybody imitated or admired. Still there were exceptions. The sturdy old master of vigorous common sense ridiculed ballads and imitators. He was accustomed to say that any one may write such verses all day long. He sustained theory by example. Boswell gives us a specimen of an extemporized imitation produced to prove the assertion. It reminds us of Goldsmith's Edwin and Angelina, although not quite as pathetic:

> Hermit hoar in solemn cell
>   Wearing out life's evening gray,
> Strike thy bosom, sage, and tell
>   Where is bliss and which the way;
> Thus he said, and saying, sighed,
>   Scarce repressed the starting tear,
> When the hoary sage replied,
>   Come my lad, and drink some beer.[11]

A very pleasant termination certainly, and much more natural than that of Chevy Chace, where men fought upon their stumps when deprived of their legs!

> When their legs were smitten off
> They fought upon their stumps.

The "Ancient Marinere," the wonder of ballads, creates the same diversity of judgment with different classes of readers. Some think it the most charming poem in the language, and are delighted with its ghastly dead men, putrid seas, and crawling abominations. Others judge it to be drawn out to a wearisome length; its hideous images produce disgust at last instead of giving them pleasure; they regard it as offending against the first principle of good poetry, according to the authority of Coleridge himself—the principle that every poem should be common sense at least.[12] They insist that whatever amount of rhyme it may contain, there is no reason whatever in a poem which represents a wedding guest as caught by a lunatic on his way to a kinsman's marriage, held by his button, during the night, within sight and hearing of the merriment, and made to listen to the long yarn of an old sailor, unable or unwilling to get away. They believe that the glittering eye, instead of fixing the guest, would assuredly have induced him to run away or call for the help of the nearest police officer, and that it would have been much more in conformity with probability to make the seizure of the unfortunate listener happen, not before, but after the festival, when being filled with wine and wassail, the maudlin carouser would have been a fit, and perhaps a willing auditor, to the lunatic old Salt.

Sir Walter Scott, as often as he read the "Vanity of human expectations," [13] shed tears of sympathy and delight over the noble and pathetic picture of common disappointment and sorrow; Wordsworth could find nothing in it worthy of remark, except a clumsy personification at the beginning.

The world of readers admire Shakspeare enthusiastically. Coleridge thinks it as impossible to displace advantageously a single word in his poetry as it is to push out a stone from one of the pyramids with one's hand,[14] although, it may be remarked in passing, commentators have been pushing these words out and in, with their pens, for more than a hundred years. Other critics, like Voltaire, describe him as a barbarous violater of the unities and other principles of the legitimate drama, and Byron and Rogers, to say nothing of inferior names, are cold in their devotions to the Bard of Avon.

We regard Milton as supreme in sublimity and beauty, "his soul is like a star that shines apart;" [15] some of the German critics class him with Klopstock and the Paradise Lost with the Messiah.

Tennyson's last poem, which, to some readers, is Tennyson's "Maud," to others is Tennyson's "Maudlin."

On the night of his attack on the heights above Quebec, while silently dropping down the stream with muffled oars, beneath the overhanging shadows of its dark and lofty banks, under all the excitement of a dangerous military movement, on the eve of a battle which changed the fortunes of a continent, General Wolfe slowly repeated the elegy in a country church yard; and now, gentlemen, he said, on concluding, I would rather be the author of this poem than to be the victor in a great battle. Others find in it nothing but borrowed phrases ingeniously dovetailed.— They think the Curfew bell was tolled by the poet at an improper hour, and consider the charge on the owl, of complaining against intrusion on her solitary reign, as signally unjust to that sweet singer of the night season, as Wordsworth considers her to be. Coleridge professed to prefer Collins to Gray, whom he affected to believe a man of taste and learning only, without imagination. Whereas, in truth, if such chimeras as the Mariner or Abyssinean maid had presented themselves to Gray's pure taste, he would have run away from them with horror and disgust.

No writer writes to all minds. No preacher is able to reach all hearts. Even Wordsworth himself affords a strong illustration of the truth of this maxim, substantially his own. He has been unduly depreciated—he has been as unreasonably praised. Some place him at the head of the writers of his age, others talk of him with slender reverence. They are even disposed to think that as the "Curse of Kehama," and "Madoc," and "Thalaba," have passed away and been forgotten, the "Prelude" and the "Excursion," the "Idiot Boy" and the "White Doe of Rylestone," will follow on the same road to oblivion; that in professing to discover a new or better way to the hill of the muses, he really bewildered himself in the fogs at its base; and that he came into the community of Poets ungraciously and ungracefully, with the air of a quack doctor in possession of a patent medicine, and not like a regular bred son of the craft. Coleridge himself, although the most partial of critics, admits that there are lines in his friend's verses absolutely intolerable—lines introduced, it would seem, as he says, for no purpose but to vindicate his peculiar principles of art.[16] We may naturally expect to find something hard and mechanical in the man, and in his works, who would set out to make poetry in the nineteenth century in conformity with a certain newly invented theory. And just so it is. He was a sort of verse making machine all his life. He lived to manufacture verses. His morning and evening walks were taken to levy poetical black mail from every stock and stone, every shrub and flower, every bird and butterfly.—The daisy that to Peter Bell was a daisy and nothing more, was to Wordsworth a very different and much more important object—it was a peg to hang verses upon. He turned over every pebble in his path to see if there might not be a stanza lurking beneath it. If he sat down on an occasional bench it produced a poem. If he visited a river it was made to rhyme. If he returned again to its banks it was forced to do double duty. Not an old thorn bush in his neighborhood escaped the general tax. Every creature within reach, asses and idiots, pedlars and prostitutes, brought grist to his indefatigable mill. He wrote with a sort of malice prepense. He walked to make verses. He traveled to make verses. He never thought of his bill but only of his rhymes. He looked on nature as a kind of poetical milch cow, which he was never tired of milking—a mass of raw material to be made up into metrical dresses. He interrogated her without ceasing, examined her minutest details, and turned every discovery to a rhyming purpose. He deals with her as a task master requiring his work to be done. He hunts up the daffodil or daisy, he does not stumble on them accidentally like Burns, when he turns one up with his plough. See, accordingly, the difference in the manner of the two writers—the words of Burns seem to gush from his heart, warm, fresh, touching in their tenderness and beauty. Wordsworth's utterances are mechanical, as if he had walked a mile with a trowel in his hand and dug up the flower over which he makes his lamentations with the express purpose to make them. There is about his poems what Coleridge calls "a matter of factness," and which he imputes to the over minuteness of the descriptions.[17] But Coleridge has not asked himself what this over minuteness proceeded from. It was itself an effect, not a cause. The whole sprung from the trade like spirit of his friend's poetry. Not that he wrote for gain. He wrote to write. It was his business, his occupation, his trade. He wrote from the eye and the head, and not, like Burns, from the heart. The verses came from him not like a stream flowing from a fountain, but like water pumped into and from a reservoir. The objects producing them were not ready witnesses volunteering a willing testimony, they were dragged into court and tortured into confession. He regarded his subjects and characters in the manner of a spectator *ab extra*—to use another phrase of Coleridge concerning him; he feels for them, not with them. He looked on nature as capability Brown,[18] the great landscape gardener, was accustomed to look, only to see what could be made of her in reference to his art. Each of them valued her as a means to accomplish an end. What is here to make a garden, asked one; what can I turn into a poem was the inquiry of the other.

In this infinite diversity of taste and judgment so obvious

to all, if a poet's claims to be free of the corporation of poets are disputed by some theoriser in essential principles, we may reply, therefore, to the assertion, that he does not please as a poet, by asking Wordsworth's question—does not please whom? The minds are infinitely varied to whom poetry is addressed. Poetry itself is endless in its forms and in its grades of merit. Parnassus is not a hill of precipitous rocky sides, like the stone mountain in Georgia, with a narrow summit, affording scanty accommodation to a few great masters of song, as some who know nothing about it affect to think. Its sides are sloping woodlands resonant with melodies and harmonies various as the songs of birds, from the chirping of the sparrow to the warbled notes of the nightingale or mocking bird, each one of them with a charm of soothing and delight for some one or other among the listeners. The great masters of song alone may occupy the summit, but every thicket and dell and bosky bourne from side to side, has its attendant melody. Let them all be enjoyed according to the hearer's taste, and carefully and reverently cherished, but let no rascal marauder enter the sacred precincts to murder or maim the humblest and gentlest of its inmates. The least pretending of the poets gives pleasure, and helps to fill up the measure of sweet sounds acceptably to some indulgent and attentive ear. One makes nature his subject, hill and valley, grove and field, flowers and trees and running streams, and the thousand sights and sounds that she presents in summer and winter, spring or autumn. Another delineates the passions that agitate the heart—love, fear, hate, revenge. Others, as Byron says, "rise to truth and moralize their song," not stoop to truth, as originally written,[19] and array their moral teachings in sonorous and attractive verse. Others scourge the vices of their times with indignant rage and scorn, like

Juvenal, or with playful severity, like Horace. Another is the poet of refinement, of wit, sense and polished society, and condenses the maxims of life in pointed, brilliant and harmonious verse. And so on without end, all deserve and may receive admiration and applause, and we may prefer one or the other without derogating from the claims of either to his own proper measure of honor and reward. All this is plain enough, so long as we are free from the bewildering phantoms of a theory. But let the critic once set up his peculiar standard of poetry, founded on what he considers the invariable principles of art, and no one can tell at what conclusions he may arrive. Instead of sound and catholic taste co-extensive with art and nature, he substitutes some narrow judgment as limited as his own views. He excludes himself from the length and breadth of nature and poetry to wall himself up in some corner of their domain, insisting that there is nothing beyond his own boundaries.

Setting aside, then, the speculations and refinements on what is supposed to be the essential principle of poetry and their mischievous consequences, let us try to arrive at a more homely and common sense, as well as comprehensive and logical answer to the question with which we began—the question, what is poetry?

It will help us in knowing what it is, to determine first what it is not. It is not, then, the nature of the thoughts expressed that makes a book a poem. It is not beauty of imagery, nor play of fancy, nor creative power of imagination, nor expression of emotion or passion, nor delineation of character, nor force, refinement or purity of language, that constitutes the *distinctive* quality of poetry. Because it is evident that there are passages in prose capable of being compared, in all these properties, not disadvantageously, with the noblest productions of the ancient or modern muse.

Take, for an example of beautiful imagery, the often quoted passage from Milton's Tractate on Education, where he expatiates on the delights of learning, "I will lead you to a hill side laborious, indeed, on the first ascent, but else so smooth, so green, so full of goodly prospects, and melodious sounds on every side, that the harp of Orpheus was not more charming," or Burke's eulogy on the adventurous hardihood of the seamen of America, or his description of the French Queen, radiant with hope and joy, at whose slightest need the sword of every gallant gentleman should have been ready to fly from its scabbard. Where in poetry shall we find invention, fancy, imagination, more abundantly exhibited than in the writings of Defoe or Fielding, or Scott or Dickens? What poet excites more readily than they do the emotions of pity or love, contempt or hatred, anger or fear. And yet, unless it be metaphorically only or to sustain a theory, no one calls Tom Jones or Robinson Crusoe or Ivanhoe a poem. The grandest example of the sublime is the simple passage from Genesis, "God said let there be light and there was light." The most exquisitely beautiful of all ethical teaching is from the sermon on the Mount, "Ye have heard that it hath been said, thou shalt love thy friends and hate thy enemies, but I say unto you, love your enemies, bless them that curse you, do good to them that hate you, and pray for them that despitefully use you and abuse you, that ye may be the children of your Father in Heaven, for He maketh his sun to shine on the evil and on the good, and sendeth his rain on the just and on the unjust." But all this is plain prose nevertheless. A prose translation of the Illiad, containing every sentiment and description faithfully expressed, would not be a poem. The passage from Milton, if turned into his own sonorous verse, would be as genuine poetry as the Comus or Paradise Lost. Turned into metrical

form by the commonest hand even, the prose is changed
into poetry, the words remaining the same.

> We lead your footsteps to a mountain's side,
> Laborious on the first ascent, but else
> So smooth, so green, so full of goodly sights,
> And sounds melodious, that the harp itself,
> Or song of Orpheus not more charming seemed.

But if it is not the thought, sentiment, imagery, either
grand or beautiful, that makes the distinctive quality of
poetry, what is it that does? If the distinguishing property
be not in the substance, it must be in the form of the work,
if not in the conceptions it must be in the words that express
them.

But the words of a language are common to poetry and
prose.

It must, then, be in the form of arranging words, that we
find the peculiar something that constitutes poetry. Coleridge defines prose to be "words in their best order," and
poetry, the "best words in the best order." [20] If he had made
the distinction to consist in the order, and not in the words,
it would be nearer the truth. For certainly the "best words"
are as fully the property of fine passages in prose as they
are of poetry. It is in the order, then, and not in the words,
that the point of distinction is to be found.—Poetry must be
defined, not from the ideas expressed, nor from the words
expressing them, but from the form in which these words
are arranged. This may be illustrated very clearly from the
passage of Milton already quoted. A slight change in the
order of the words changes it from prose to poetry.

As all language is the articulate expression of thought or
emotion, so every language recognizes two forms of expressing them—one more free and loose called prose, and
one, more restricted and subjected to certain rules, called

poetry. This is the universal law of expressing thought in all languages. Poetry is nothing more than one of the grand divisions of articulate sounds, found among all cultivated nations, and designated by similar terms. There are but two, and so Milton asks the muse to aid him in telling things un-attempted yet in prose or rhyme, meaning that they had never been attempted in any form at all. The certain rules to which, as we say above, the poetic form of expressing thought or emotion is subjected, are rules of metre and rythm. They exist in similar forms in all languages. We may, therefore, define poetry to be the expression, by words, of thought or emotion, in conformity with metrical and rythmi-cal laws.

Each of these great divisions of language is co-extensive with the limits of human thought and emotion. The whole compass of man's mind and heart is within the reach of either. Poetry is confined to no such whimsical boundaries as those of Mr. Bowles. It is true there are subjects more suitable to one mode of expression than the other, and it would indicate a want of taste and judgment to mistake in the use of one or the other as the topic may require. But the error would in nowise touch the validity of the distinction between them. It may be true, for example, that prose is more suitable than poetry for the exposition of a philosophi-cal system, and Lucretius may have been injudicious in ex-pounding the doctrines of Epicurus in any other form than prose; but no one ever doubts that his work is a poem. It may be said that the fine descriptive passages, and not the metaphysics, constitute the poetry. But no critic has yet undertaken to maintain that certain portions of the work are not poetry at all. And yet, if we abandon the only solid and true distinction between prose and poetry, and discriminate between this and that passage as poetry or not poetry, in reference to the ideas expressed, and not to the form of expression, we shall be compelled to cut up this and every long poem into slips of alternate poetry and non-poetry, according to the images and thoughts which we find in them. The Illiad will then be a poem, where Achilles shouts from the ramparts, and puts to flight the advancing and victorious Trojans by the terrors of his voice alone; or, where Helen is represented on the walls of Troy, describing to Priam, and naming the chiefs of the Grecian hosts arrayed on the plain below; but it will be no poem where, in the catalogue, the names of tribes, cities, chiefs and countries, are enumerated. The Paradise Lost will be a poem where Satan calls to his fallen multitudes, weltering in the fiery gulf confounded, though immortal—or where the charms of Paradise or the beauty and grace of Eve are described; but not where, in long discussions, the poet makes "God the father turn a school divine." [21] And so of every long poem in every language.

So, too, in all the great prose writings of every country, we shall find long passages which are to be considered poetry, the purpose of the authors to write prose only, to the contrary notwithstanding.

But those who are jealous of the dignity of poetry, and who carry in their memories and imaginations the brilliant rhetorical descriptions of the art found among poets and orators, are not content with being told that the art of poetry is a mere form of expressing thought. And yet what higher account can be given of poetry than this, that it is the noblest, most refined, pointed and energetic of the two modes by which among all people, thought and emotion are expressed by language. Language itself is something wonderful. It is the gift of God. All that poets and orators say of poetry may be said of language. It is a divine art, and of this divine art the poets are masters of the highest form. The greater the artist, the greater his mastery in this instrument, by which he rules the hearts and minds of men. Homer paints with a word. Virgil's style or diction is inimitable. To Horace belongs the *curiosa felicitas* of words.[22] In Milton and Shakspeare, according to Coleridge, you cannot alter a word without spoiling a line. To be the master of this wonderful power in any form, divinely imparted as it is, confers high distinction—to be its master, in its noblest form, makes the poet's honor and constitutes his art.

If we are met with the question, what, then, are we to consider as poetry the metrical lines, assigning its number of days to each month, or shall we class the stanzas extemporized by Johnson as such? We would meet the one question by another—are we to regard the chat at a corner, or the plain talk of a laborer, or the slang of a pot house, as prose? In either case there is a wide interval between the lowest and highest specimens of the two divisions of language—between the doggerel and Comus, between the slang and Burke—but not more so in the one than in the other. The question as respects both refers not to the triviality of the thing expressed, but to the form of expression, and the answer in both must be the same.

But it is said again, the ordinary phrases of conversation intimate a difference between poetry and mere verse—we say of a clumsy poet, that he is a mere versifier, and of a dull poem, that it is no better than prose. But we are not to understand this as meaning that the writer is not a poet and his work not a poem. Such phrases mean only that the poet and poem are deficient in vivacity or vigor, or refinement and finish. It is a criticism which touches the execution and not the form of the work. We say of a tedious talker that he is prosy or a proser, but we do not mean that he is speaking something different from prose. So, we say of a man that he is effeminate or womanlike, or an ass, or a mule or a fox, or a tiger, but in no case do we intend to say that he is not a man. We propose only to designate the qualities or character of the party, and not the sex or genus to which he belongs. The critic, however, seizes on these figurative expressions, in reference to poetry, and turns the whole subject into confusion by mistaking and confounding two questions essentially different—the one asking to what category of expression a work belongs, the other what degree of merit it may possess; one inquiring into its nature, the other into its merits.

When from asking whether a book is a poem, we turn to examine into its faults and beauties, the whole province of inquiry is changed. The critic may lavish upon it any amount of disparaging names that his nomenclature happens to include. It may be dull, stupid, prosaic, but he can by no means convert it into prose. We can allow him any latitude of censure, but we protest against his giving point to his censure by confounding all logical distinction in the modes of expressing thought. A bad poem is still a poem, the most excellent prose is still prose, and the landmarks must remain undisturbed by the conflicting parties.

The department of literature to which a writer belongs, will not depend on the subject treated, but on the form of expression in which he treats it; in making poetry to consist in the noblest form of language, itself so noble a distinction of man, we in no respect derogate from the dignity of the art, it is the noblest form of that noble faculty without which thought itself would perish or be deprived of its wings.

Notes

and

Index

The Character and Scope of the Sonnet

1 "The Character and Scope of the Sonnet" was published in *Russell's Magazine*, I: 156-59 (May, 1857). It was reprinted in *The Outlook*, LXXVII: 706-9 (July 23, 1904). The editor in an introductory note praises Timrod as poet and as critic, and erroneously claims that he is publishing the article for the first time. This version twice breaks one paragraph into two, and omits quotation marks from "the hour of insight" and from "stature reaches the sky." Otherwise, except for slight changes in punctuation, the two versions are identical.

2 Milton, *Paradise Lost*, VII, 31: "fit audience find, though few."

3 *Recollections of the Table-Talk of Samuel Rogers*, New York, 1856, p. 207.

4 Quotation not located.

5 Wordsworth, "Observations Prefixed to 'Lyrical Ballads'": "I have said that poetry is the spontaneous overflow of powerful feelings: it takes its origin from emotion recollected in tranquillity."

6 Wordsworth, *The Prelude*, I, 233.

7 Wordsworth, *The Prelude*, I, 46-47: "not used to make / A present joy the matter of a song."

8 Arnold, "Morality," stanza 1. The italics are Timrod's.

9 Aubrey de Vere, "Sorrow."

10 Milton, *Paradise Lost*, IV, 988.

Timrod's "What is Poetry?"

[1] Timrod's "What is Poetry?" was published in *Russell's Magazine*, II: 52-58 (October, 1857). The "writer in the July number" is Grayson; since his essay is re-printed in this book, the reader can compare Timrod's lengthy quotations with Grayson's entire argument.

I have corrected the following typographical errors: in ¶ 23, semetimes: sometimes; in the last ¶, Laodimia: Laodamia.

[2] See the "Definition of Poetry" at the beginning of the 1836 edition of "Literary Remains," or "Shakspeare, with introductory matter on Poetry, the Drama, and the Stage": "Poetry is not the proper antithesis to prose, but to science. Poetry is opposed to science, and prose to metre." Timrod may also be referring to Coleridge's famous definition, in the *Biographia Literaria*, Ch. XIV: "A poem is that species of composition, which is opposed to works of science, by proposing for its *immediate* object, pleasure, not truth." In this chapter and in XVIII, Coleridge discusses the problem of metre as opposed to prose. See note eleven.

[3] In his "Observations Prefixed to 'Lyrical Ballads,'" Wordsworth writes: "I have said that poetry is the spontaneous overflow of powerful feelings: it takes its origin from emotion recollected in tranquillity: the emotion is contemplated till, by a species of reaction, the tranquillity gradually disappears, and an emotion, kindred to that which was before the subject of contemplation, is gradually produced, and does itself actually exist in the mind."

Shelley, in "A Defence of Poetry," wrote that "Poetry is the record of the best and happiest moments of the happiest and best minds."

[4] Coleridge, *Biographia Literaria*, Ch. XIV.

[5] Arthur Henry Hallam, "On Some of the Characteristics of Modern Poetry and on the Lyrical Poems of Alfred Tennyson," in the *Remains in Prose and Verse of Arthur Henry Hallam with a Memoir*, edited by Henry Hallam (London, 1863), pp. 304-305.

[6] Timrod is adapting to his own argument, with some changes, Milton's definition of poetry ("Letter to Samuel Hartlib: On Education," frequently called the "Tractate on Education," 1644) as being "more simple, sensuous, and passionate" than logic and rhetoric.

NOTES 159

7 Shakspere, *Antony and Cleopatra*, V, 2, 88-90. See note 16, "A Theory of Poetry."

8 Coleridge, *Table Talk*, July 12, 1827: "I wish our clever young poets would remember my homely definitions of prose and poetry; that is, prose —words in their best order; poetry—the best words in their best order."

9 "Prose and Song," in *The Poetical Works of John Sterling* (Philadelphia, 1842), 232.

10 Coleridge, *Biographia Literaria*, Ch. XIV: "In short, whatever specific import we attach to the word, Poetry, there will be found involved in it, as a necessary consequence, that a poem of any length, neither can be, nor ought to be, all poetry. Yet if an harmonious whole is to be produced, the remaining parts must be preserved in keeping with the poetry; and this can be no otherwise effected than by such a studied selection and artificial arrangement, as will partake of one, though not a peculiar property of poetry."

11 The Coleridge reference is given in note 2. In the second footnote in "Observations Prefixed to 'Lyrical Ballads,'" Wordsworth writes: "I here use the word 'Poetry' (though against my own judgement) as opposed to the word Prose, and synonymous with metrical composition. But much confusion has been introduced into criticism by this contradistinction of Poetry and Prose, instead of the more philosophical one of Poetry and Matter of Fact, or Science. The only strict antithesis to Prose is Metre; nor is this, in truth, a *strict* antithesis, because lines and passages of metre so naturally occur in writing prose, that it would be scarcely possible to avoid them, even were it desirable."

12 See Lamb's "Imperfect Sympathies," in *Essays of Elia*.

13 Coleridge, *Biographia Literaria*, Chapters XIV and XVIII.

14 Wordsworth, *The Excursion*, I, 213: "Thought was not; in enjoyment it expired." In this and the quotation from "Tintern Abbey," the italics are Timrod's. He omits two parenthetical lines from "Tintern Abbey," and his punctuation differs slightly from the Oxford text in both quotations from that poem.

15 Coleridge, *Biographia Literaria*, Ch. XXII. For the next paragraph, see the same chapter, and Ruskin's *Modern Painters*, Part III, Sec. 2, Ch. 4.

16 Wordsworth, Poem IV of "Poems on the Naming of Places," the first line beginning, "A narrow girdle of rough stones and crags." The italics are Timrod's; the punctuation differs from the Oxford text; and in the last line, "Lone-sitting" should be "Sole-sitting."

Literature in the South

[1] "Literature in the South" was first published in *Russell's Magazine*, V: 385-95 (August, 1859). It probably served also as a speech at Cheraw, South Carolina; in the *Courant*, a magazine published at Columbia, H. H. Caldwell wrote a brief paragraph (I, 1, May 5, 1859): "We see in the Cheraw papers accounts of the Lecture of Henry Timrod, our young Carolina Petrarch, who has been holding forth on 'The Southern Author.' "

For a good survey of this general subject, see Jay B. Hubbell's "Literary Nationalism in the Old South," in *American Studies in Honor of William Kenneth Boyd*, Durham, 1940, pp. 175-220.

I have made the following typographical changes: ¶8, Thompson: Thomson; ¶12, carollary: corollary; Theories has: theories have; ¶21, Maryatt: Marryatt.

[2] Shakspere, *Henry IV*, Part I, II, iv, 42-90.

[3] Undoubtedly William Gilmore Simms. Timrod's own attitude toward Simms varied. On Feb. 9, 1860, Hayne wrote Simms asking for a review of Timrod's *Poems:* "When leisure and inclination coincide, will you not oblige *me* by a brief review of Timrod's Poems? I know, after what has occurred, *he* can urge *no possible* claim upon your notice" (W. P. Trent, *William Gilmore Simms*, p. 233). Trent remarks that Timrod was highly critical of Simms' poetry and poetical views, but he also quotes from a letter apparently no longer extant (p. 297: Timrod to Simms): "Somehow or other, you always magnetize me on to a little strength." For other examples of Timrod's impatience with Simms, see his letters to Hayne in J. B. Hubbell's *The Last Years of Henry Timrod*, pp. 54 and 82-84. Worth noting as significant in this relationship, however, are two items that appeared in the columns of the *Daily South Carolinian* (May 3, 1864, and Aug. 7, 1864) during Timrod's editorship, and almost certainly written by him. They show an unaffected cordiality. The first item is here given in full: "We had the pleasure of welcoming to our office, yesterday, WILLIAM GILMORE SIMMS, Esq., poet, critic, novelist, historian, and one of the oldest living editors of the South. No man has done half so much as this wondrously prolific writer to create a Southern literature, whether by the achievements of his own broad genius or by the generous encouragement which he has lavished upon younger aspirants. No name

shines forth more brightly on the pages of letters than his, and unquestionably there is no brain on this continent that has labored more assiduously and successfully to transmit to posterity the great lessons of the past and present.

"Mr. SIMMS has been and will continue to be, a contributor to our columns."

The second speaks of Simms as "Brimming over with delightful talk, showering his golden thoughts on every hearer, uttering more philosophy in half an hour than would suffice to fill a respectable volume, striking or startling all around with the profundity and originality of his observations, scattering curious and recondite information with a lavish hand, full of genius and sense and spirit . . ."

4 Hugh Blair (1718-1800) published his widely used *Lectures on Rhetoric and Belles-Lettres* in two volumes at Edinburgh, 1783. An American edition was published in Philadelphia in 1784. After 1787, the work was frequently re-published, usually in three volumes.

5 Probably a typographical error. Henry Home, Lord Kames (1696-1782) published his three-volume *Elements of Criticism* at Edinburgh, 1762. It was twice revised and enlarged (1763, 1788), and was reprinted many times.

6 Even in the emotionalism that was prevalent during the Civil War, Timrod held steadfastly to this idea. Shortly after he became an editor of the Columbia *Daily South Carolinian*, Timrod published an editorial that in part repeats his essay (Jan. 19, 1864):

By nationality in literature, we do not mean simply the choice of subjects peculiar to the country of the writer. It would be quite possible for a Southern poet to write a hundred odes to the Confederate flag, or for a Southern novelist to fill his book with descriptions of Southern scenes, and yet to be un-Southern in every respect. If, in the construction of plot or poem, a trace of foreign models appear, we must deny the author all right to be considered as national in the true sense of the word.

On the other hand, an author may travel a thousand miles away from home, yet, nevertheless, preserve his nationality. Shakspeare wandered to Rome, and Scott to Palestine, each without losing his title to rank as a representative writer of his nation.

We have been led to these remarks, from the consideration of a very common error among the critics of the South. This error consists in supposing what we have just denied, that an author is Southern, in proportion as his lyrics relate to the South, and his thought and imagery are drawn from Southern sources. In the opinion of these philosophers, all his trees should be palmettoes, and all his fields white with cotton.

The question really lies in a nut shell. There is but one way to be a truly national writer, and that is by being a truly original writer. No one who does not speak from himself can speak for his country, and, therefore, no imitator can be national. But the man of original genius draws his matter from the depth of his own being; and the national character, in which, as a unit of the nation, he shares, finds its utterance through him without his will. It is of no consequence, in his case, into what century, or what *ultima thule,* he may stray; he will still carry with him those characteristics which he imbibed from the national influences around him. And wherever he may lay the scenes of his stories, it shall so happen, that, without violating a single propriety of place or climate, the pines of his own forest shall be heard to murmur, his own rivers shall roll in music, the flowers of his own soil, touched perhaps with a more lasting and ethereal grace, shall shed their perfume over his pages, and his own skies will look down upon the loveliest landscapes of his creation.

We must not be understood in the above remarks to mean anything inconsistent with the necessities of dramatic characterization. The Romans of Shakspeare are all Romans, and when that great poet ventriloquises through the person of Antony, he does not permit the tones of Shakspeare to be heard. Nevertheless, even in his Roman plays, the English qualities of his genius are apparent in the muscular strength of his style, and in that very power, which the writers of no nation have displayed to such a degree as those of England, of putting off his own character and assuming that of another.

We conclude with a brief word to the young authors of the South. Let them not be too careful to confine themselves to Southern [*sic*] topics. If they are led by some inner inspiration, and not by the mere caprice of choice, they may find, even amid the Arctic ice, or the luminous seas of the tropics, spots upon which they may plant, never to be taken down, the flag of their country's genius!

⁷ In 1864, Timrod thought that intellectual independence might be forced upon the South (*Daily South Carolinian,* Jan. 14, 1864):

The great and troubled movement through which we are passing has stirred the Southern mind to an unwonted activity. No pre-eminently great man, indeed, has arisen amid the turmoil, but the people are beginning to think with an independence which they never evinced in their former provincial position.

It is with reference to literature only that we wish to speak briefly of this improvement in the national character. It is an improvement which, in the department of letters, at least, we owe to the very blockade that has cut off so completely our supplies of Northern and of English books. Forced to supply ourselves, we have, also, learned to criticise without regard to foreign models, and criticism in growing independent has likewise become sensible.

Our authors are waking up to the fact that they have at last an audience. More novels, histories, and poems have been written at the South within the last two years than within any previous ten. Most of these, doubtless, have been of merit sufficiently indifferent, but still some of them have been clever, and all tend to show that a new era of intellectual energy is dawning upon us. . . .

⁸ Timrod used this same figure effectively in "The Cotton Boll":

> To the remotest point of sight,
> Although I gaze upon no waste of snow,
> The endless field is white;

Timrod also uses this figure in "Ethnogenesis."

⁹ John Playfair (1748-1819), *Outlines of Natural Philosophy*, 2 vols., London, 1812-14.

¹⁰ Coleridge, *Biographia Literaria*, Ch. I.

¹¹ At least a partial change in sentiment, and a public demand for one kind of poetry, was the subject of an editorial by Timrod in the Columbia *Daily South Carolinian*, Jan. 24, 1864:

A short while ago, everybody was calling for a national song. The few poets who are to be found in the Confederacy, were importuned to write one, and many attempts to supply the want were made, both by poets and poetasters, without the slightest success. Good and bad poems were written, but none, with the exception of "My Maryland," and that only for a little time, touched the heart of the people so deeply as to become one of its representative [sic] songs.

We are not to blame our poets for this failure. A nation does not choose its songs on the ground of poetical merit. In fact, it does not choose them at all. It is impossible to trace where a song begins its career of popularity, and its diffusion throughout a nation depends upon some fortunate conjunction of time, mood, association, and circumstance. Judging from the character and history of the few established poems of this kind which we possess, there are but four things necessary to the success of an attempt to write a national song. Its verse must run glibly on the tongue; it must contain somewhere, either in a stanza or a refrain, a sentiment, tersely and musically expressed, which appeals to some favorite pride, prejudice or passion of the people; it must be married to an effective, but not complicated air, and it must be aided by such a collocation of accidents as may not be computed.

If the above essentials are not wanting, it little matters, so far as popularity is concerned, whether the song as a whole, be worthless, in a literary point of view or not. The "Star Spangled Banner" is utterly destitute of every thing that deserves the name of poetry. But it was commended to the popular heart by its refrain, which embodies in a form concise and sounding enough, the Yankee's pride in his country. "Rule Britannia" also owes it rank as a national song to the chorus alone; the rest of the poem, although the song was written by the author of the "Castle of Indolence," being the merest fustian.

The reader will understand, that we have been speaking of what national songs have been, not what they ought to be. A national song which would be worthy of the name—a song in which the poet should express the whole great soul of a nation within the compass of a few simple and melodious verses—enclosing, like the enchanters of Eastern story, a giant within the cup of a lily—such a song would imply, in its composition, a genius not less than that which wrote Paradise Lost. We have, indeed, at this day, no poets who are equal to production of this lofty character. Nevertheless, there are not wanting, in the Confederate States, a few genuine children of song, and we would be glad to see them renewing their efforts in this direction. Surely, in the present situation of their country, struggling for its liberties against overpowering odds, and isolated from the rest of the world—a situation more full of pathos and grandeur than anything in Greek or Roman story—they ought to find inspiration enough to draw forth the utmost capacity of their genius. If they are true to their duty and their vocation—if they can catch the spirit which wakes our blood-stained valleys with shouts of battle, and which goes forth in words of unconquerable cheer from our desolated hearths, they may yet accomplish among them a song, which, however, it may fall short of the ideal to which we have briefly alluded, may stir the heart more than the roar of a thousand patriot cannon!

[12] Coleridge, *Biographia Literaria*, Ch. XV.

[13] Sir Henry Taylor, in Preface to *Philip Van Artevelde*.

[14] This also, Timrod thought in 1864, might be brought about by the war (Columbia *Daily South Carolinian*, Jan. 15, 1864):

Everybody remembers how difficult a thing it was, before the war, to establish and keep up a Southern periodical. Now periodicals are springing up like daisies in every direction, and, what is more, with all the hardiness of those little field flowers, they seem destined to live and flourish for some time. This success is not simply owing to the fact that Southern magazines, having no longer to contend with Northern publications, are devoured for the want of other and better reading. The Southern mind is aroused, and in its awakening energies there is a reciprocity of action between the writers and readers. As readers increase, so do writers, and the reverse is also true. Moreover, the nationality of the Southern people is becoming, under the influence of passing events, more and more sharply defined, and that nationality begins to demand an expression of its own. Any attempt, however feeble, to satisfy this demand will meet with encouragement and support. . . .

[15] Frances Trollope, *Domestic Manners of the Americans* (1832); Charles Dickens, *American Notes for General Circulation* (1842); Frederick Marryatt, *A Diary in America, with Remarks on its Institutions* (1839); Basil Hall, *Travels in North America in the years 1827 and 1828* (1829). Dickens and Trollope gave especial offence to Southerners by their disparaging remarks on the region.

[16] Robert Pollok's (1789-1827) *The Course of Time* (1827) was a ten-book poem in blank verse, on spiritual life and the destiny of man. Twelve thousand copies were sold in the first eighteen months; the 25th edition appeared in 1867.

A Theory of Poetry

[1] "A Theory of Poetry" was delivered as a lecture before the Methodist Female College, Columbia, S. C., in the winter of 1863-64. Timrod's widow, Mrs. Kate Goodwin Timrod Lloyd, wrote to W. A. Courtenay that she could not find the exact date of the lecture, "But I am quite sure it was some time in 63—before we were married, but were engaged. He handed me the manuscript, which I gave you, as he left the rostrum. It was given in aid of the poor soldiers who as you will well know were in a most deplorable condition, half starved, and half-clothed." (Letter, March 7, 1901, bound in *Memories of the Timrod Revival*, Charleston Library Society). In an earlier letter (March 15, 1898), Mrs. Lloyd had mentioned the manuscript, and said that the *Century* had declined it because of its length.

The manuscript is now in the Charleston Library Society; since it is exactly as Timrod wrote it, I have used it as the best text. It is quite legible, written in ink, and needs very little editing. No title is given on the manuscript; stamped on the binding is the title, "An Essay on Poetry." Since this seems to have no more validity than the title by which the essay is generally known, I have kept the title, "A Theory of Poetry."

After receiving the manuscript, Courtenay had the pages carefully pasted within heavy cut-out pages (Timrod had written on both sides of the paper) and sumptuously bound. From this original a manuscript was prepared for magazine publication before 1901. Many changes, but very few improvements, were made by this unknown editor, and no indication of changes was given. The worst feature of the editing was to remove something of Timrod's individuality and force; to make his style conform more to the ordinary magazine style of the year 1900, and in that way to make his work seem more stereotyped than it was.

Apparently the essay was not published until 1901, when it was printed in a slightly abridged form in *The Independent*, the first installment entitled "A Theory of Poetry," LIII: 712-16, March 28, 1901; the second and third installments, "The Rationale of Poetry," LIII: 760-64, 830-33, April 4 and April 11, 1901. An introductory note signed H. A. (Henry Austin) praises Timrod as a poet and critic whose reputation is rising, and explains that the essay has been slightly edited: the sentences referring to occasion of delivery deleted (actually, the first three paragraphs), occasional missing conjunctives supplied, quotations and historical facts corrected. Austin notes as one error Timrod's statement that Poe was born in the South, and takes occasion to claim Poe as "Boston's most distinguished and hitherto unappreciated son." The introductory note to Part II explains that Timrod had no adequate edition of Poe, but most of the distortion of Poe's phrasing is only in the magazine version, and not in Timrod's manuscript.

"A Theory of Poetry" was re-printed without any reference to earlier publication in the *Atlantic Monthly*, XCVI: 313-26, September, 1905. It restores the three opening paragraphs, but otherwise does not differ materially from the earlier printed version.

A pencilled paragraph by Timrod above the body of the essay was used as an introduction for a second lecture. This paragraph is given here, as not belonging to the essay itself:

"It is with considerable hesitation that I chose the subject of the essay which I read for the second time to-night. It was so familiar that I thought I might well distrust my ability to give it interest. Yet I shall go over it with less diffidence than last night—because I address the gentler sympathies and less cautious criticism of a more youthful audience. Moreover, I repeat what I said then."

The essay was prepared as a speech. The punctuation was intended to aid the writer in speaking, and not to aid a reader unfamiliar with it; but Timrod's punctuation is certainly no more confusing than that of his editor. For this book, where words or marks of punctuation have seemed absolutely necessary, these have been added in brackets; two of Timrod's deletions are given in the appropriate notes; in ¶10, Timrod had written *point*, and above it *fact*, without any deleting—I have used *point* in the text; and the following obvious corrections have been made: ¶3, synonomous: synonymous; ¶8, pschyal: psychal; is is: as is; ¶11, the the: one *the* deleted; ¶11, dusky is written over and is indistinct. This seems the best reading; ¶11, famility: familiar; quotation marks omitted after brooks; ¶14, comprend: comprehend; ¶16, quotation marks removed before Great Pack, since they were not closed; ¶18, what what: one *what* deleted; ¶22, one who . . . sit: sits; quotation marks deleted after "insight," as Timrod had himself deleted them before "hour;" ¶27, proceeded: preceded; inaccuries: inaccuracies; that that couching: one *that* deleted; appearance: appearances; ¶28, Thompson: Thomson.

² Tennyson, "Two Voices," 1. 180.

³ Timrod is referring to Grayson's "What is Poetry?", which is re-printed in this book.

⁴ Apparently Timrod cut the manuscript after ". . . years ago." As originally written, and partly crossed out, the paragraph read: "The second theory which I desire to examine critically was propounded a number of years ago by the most exquisite poetical genius to which the South has yet given birth. It seems to me an exceedingly narrow one, but yet it is so full of beautiful half-truths, and is supported with so much skill and eloquence, that on many it exercises a dangerous fascination. I allude to the 'Poetic Principle' of Poe. I will not fear that I shall be accused of presumption in assailing it, because the only boldness of which I am conscious is that of an earnest faith, and of a passionate and studious love of the essence and the art of Poetry."

All of Timrod's quotations from Poe are from "The Poetic Principle." There are slight inaccuracies and omissions, but in no instance is Poe's thought distorted. In the next paragraph, Timrod first wrote, "excitements are, though a psychal necessity, transient." Apparently he then attempted to jam an *r* in front of the *o*, to make the word *through*, as it should be. The *o* is heavily inked and blurred.

⁵ Charles Lamb, "Detached Thoughts on Books and Reading," in *Last Essays of Elia* (1833): "Milton almost requires a solemn service of music to be played before you enter upon him. But he brings his music, to which, who listens, had need bring docile thoughts, and purged ears."

⁶ *The Beauties of Shakspear*, edited by William Dodd (1729-77), 2 vols. London, 1752. See Coleridge, *Biographia Literaria*, Ch. III.

⁷ *Paradise Lost*, IV, 238. In the next line, "Flowers of all hues" is from Book IV, 256. The lines at the end of the paragraph are at the close of the poem; the last line should be "Through Eden took their solitarie way."

⁸ This quotation was an after-thought, and was crowded in between two lines; not located.

⁹ Byron, *Childe Harold's Pilgrimage*, Canto IV, Stanza CLV. The punctuation differs slightly from that of the standard text.

¹⁰ Joel Barlow's *Columbiad* (1807).

¹¹ Coleridge, *Biographia Literaria*, Ch. XIV. An interlinear addition. The quotation is given in note 10, Timrod's "What is Poetry?".

¹² Wordsworth, "Observations Prefixed to 'Lyrical Ballads,'" and Shelley, "A Defence of Poetry." See note 3, Timrod's "What is Poetry?".

¹³ At this point the following sentences were evidently cut during the composition of the essay: "It is indeed to a sort of discontent with the un-realities and imperfections of earth, and in the perception of a higher existence than the life which we actually lead, that the world owes the inspiration of some of the noblest poems in its possession. The sentiment of poetry as it thus developed in the mind is the very ground on which (apart from Revelation) we base our hopes of immortality, and this fact should make it the next sacred thing to the great Chart of Salvation."

14 *Paradise Lost*, I, 294: "the Mast / Of some great ammiral"—*i.e.*, the ship that carries the admiral. Later in this sentence, Timrod interlined "the orient" above the word "India," but did not delete the latter; the phrase "of ships" was deleted after the word "wrecks."

15 Wordsworth, "A Poet's Epitaph," l. 49: "In common things that round us lie."

16 Leigh Hunt, *Imagination and Fancy, or Selections from the English Poets, illustrative of those First Requisites of their Art; with Markings of the Best Passages, Critical Notices of the Writers, and an Essay in answer to the Question, "What is Poetry?"*, 1844.

17 Shakspere, *Antony and Cleopatra*, V, 2, 88-90:

> His delights
> Were dolphin like; they show'd his back above
> The element they lived in

I have added quotation marks after *in*, in accordance with Timrod's usage.

18 The preceding lines, beginning with "the hour of patient and elaborate execution," were lightly underscored in pencil, possibly as a guide to emphasis in reading. A few phrases were not underscored.

19 See Poe's "The Philosophy of Composition."

20 Wordsworth, *The Prelude*, I, l. 47. See note 7 on "The Sonnet." The strength of Timrod's belief in this is best illustrated in two editorials published in war-time:

WAR AND LITERATURE

It is not during the present war, (the Atlanta *Confederacy*, and its eloquent appeal to the writers of the day, notwithstanding,) that we can look for any great achievements in literature. Thought now flows mainly but in one channel, and boils along, in too turbulent a stream to be confined within the limitations of polished prose or harmonious verse. To the poet this remark is particularly applicable. No greater error prevails, than the very common one of supposing that a state of excitement is favorable to the production of poetry. The contrary, indeed, is the fact. WORDS-WORTH'S definition of poetry, as "emotion recollected in tranquility," though, doubtless, especially characteristic of his own works, is yet also true, to a great extent, with regard to every genuine votary of song. A certain amount of composure is always necessary to the composition of a poem. What emotion is felt during the composition, is not the grief or joy to which the poet is attempting to give expression, but that grief or joy idealized by the influences of imagination and of time. One would suppose, however, from the manner in which most people talk of the subject, that no sooner does a poet feel the rapture of a successful love, than he bursts at once into anapæsts, and that, in the depths of his profoundest despair, he is prepared to tell his sorrow in quatrains that shall sound like a passing bell. If this were so, he would be the most wonderful of improvisatores. But, as we have already said, such is not the case. Very rarely does the poet make a present feeling the matter of his song. It is only when that feeling has become somewhat subdued, and when he has had time to brood over its operations in his soul, that he proceeds to embody it in the music of his verse. Hence it is, that we need not look to see the stormy emotions of the struggle through which we are passing, reduced immediately to song. Peace must bring its soothing influences before the poet, who shares with all of us the agitation of the strife, can regain that calm which the practice of his art demands.

While, however, the tumult of revolution is undoubtedly incompatible with the composition of poetry, it operates, on the other hand, not without much salutary effect upon the poetical genius. In the very excitement which seals for awhile the poet's lips, he is receiving an education which shall bear the noblest fruits in the future. With a soul strengthened and elevated by the grand emotions which have stirred its profoundest depths, and with a mind filled with recollections of the deeds of heroism and self-sacrifice which he has witnessed, he will be the better able hereafter to breathe into his works the whole spirit of that period, the disturbing elements of which have only imposed a temporary silence upon his muse.

Convinced of the truth of the above remarks, we are not among those who are disposed to complain of the present apparent inactivity of the poetical mind. It is our firm belief that in the brain of every true poet of the Confederacy sleeps many a poem, which, though it may not burst into blossom, until the return of peace, shall show in the color of all its petals that its roots are deep in the blood-enriched soil of the now pending revolution. (*Daily South Carolinian,* Columbia, February 28, 1864.)

· · · ·
(*no heading*)

We noticed not long ago, in one of our exchanges, a complaint that the war had produced no poetry likely to live beyond the present generation. This sweeping assertion is unjust to at least a dozen fine lyrics that we could name; yet there is no doubt that the stormy emotions of the time have not found any very general expression in verse. This fact however, would not surprise us if we only remembered that in these latter days of the world, at least, war has never produced much poetry. At a period when cruel commotion was staining the daisies of England with the blood of her best and bravest men, there lived one of the greatest poets that ever achieved an immortality upon earth. Yet, though warmly enlisted in the contest, and though he contributed a great deal of glorious prose to the cause which he espoused, he has left scarcely a single line of verse which would indicate that he had not written in the midst of the profoundest peace. There was nothing Tyrtœan in the author of Paradise Lost. Again, when that same England was summoning all her energies and tasking all her strength to crush the first Emperor of the French, there flourished within her borders such a chorus of poets as, except "in the spacious time of great ELIZABETH," the world had never heard. But while the mighty struggle that was going on had its influence upon the tone and character of their thoughts, these poets nevertheless drew their inspiration mainly from the more peaceful influences around them. Other instances might be adduced, but the above are enough to show that war, in spite of the virtues which it developes and the emotions which it stirs, does not readily obtain representation in poetry, even where there is no deficiency of poetical genius. The explanation of the fact must be left to the metaphysical critic; but we may suggest that it may partly be found in the meditative character of the poets and poetry of the present age. The poet of the nineteenth century is a philosopher, and the poetry of the nineteenth century is marked rather by thought than passion. Hence we have but few such bursts of mere martial enthusiasm as the Marseillaise Hymn in the poetical literature of the day. We need not look, therefore for more than an occasional poem of this kind from the South. (Sept. 15, 1864.)

[21] Wordsworth, *The Excursion*, I, ll. 105-6: "The high and tender Muses shall accept / With gracious smile, deliberately pleased." The "Orphean lyre" is in *The Prelude*, I, l. 233. I have completed the quotation marks after lyre. The italics are Timrod's.

[22] Arnold, "Morality," stanza 1. The italics are Timrod's.

[23] Francis Bacon, *Of the Advancement of Learning*, Book II (1605): "So as it appeareth that poesy serveth and conferreth to magnanimity, morality, and delectation." (p. 88 of *The Philosophical Works of Francis Bacon*, edited by John M. Robertson, 1905). *Works of Francis Bacon*, London, 1826, VII, p. 128, gives the Latin of the 1622 version: Adeo ut poësis ista, non solum ad delectationem, sed etiam ad animi magnitudinem, et ad mores conferat.

[24] Coleridge, *Biographia Literaria*, Ch. XV.

[25] Wordsworth, "Observations Prefixed to 'Lyrical Ballads.' "

[26] Cf. "Tintern Abbey," ll. 95 ff. Quotation not located.

[27] Tennyson became Poet Laureate in 1850, succeeding Wordsworth.

[28] Wordsworth, *The Excursion*, Preface, ll. 42-55. The punctuation and capitalization vary from that of the Oxford edition. Likewise, the quotation from "Tintern Abbey" (ll. 75-102) shows some divergences.

[29] Coleridge, "To William Wordsworth," ll. 46-48, in *Sybilline Leaves*.

[30] Wordsworth, *Poems of the Imagination*, VIII. The only deviation of any importance is in the last line. It should read: "With something of angelic light." Final quotation marks added.

[31] Tennyson, "The Day-Dream," ll. 201-204.

[32] Tennyson, *The Princess*, Part ii, l. 165 (Student's Cambridge Edition, 1898). Timrod wrote "the blood the blood."

[33] Wordsworth, "Personal Talk," ll. 51-54:

> Blessings be with them—and eternal praises,
> Who gave us nobler loves, and nobler cares—
> The Poets, who on earth have made us heirs
> Of truth and pure delight by heavenly lays!

The following sentence at the end was evidently written in as an after-thought and then rejected: "I do not counsel the rejection of a single favourite but desire only that that favourite should not furnish the rules by which you measure the merits of the most dissimilar productions."

,

Grayson's "What is Poetry?"

[1] Grayson's "What is Poetry?" was published in *Russell's Magazine*, I: 327-37 (July, 1857). The essay was one part of his defence of eighteenth-century poetry; it was the work of an older man who found himself unsympathetic to the ideas and work of the Romantic poets.

William John Grayson was born at Beaufort, South Carolina, on Nov. 12, 1788. After attending various private schools in his home town, in New York and in Newark, he entered South Carolina College as a sophomore on Feb. 7, 1807, and graduated Dec. 7, 1809. Of his college days he remembered later that he and James L. Petigru spent a summer night "over the wild wit of Rabelais," and that daylight found them "engaged in the coarse but irresistible merriment of the modern master of broad humor and boisterous wit." More decorously, but with equal enthusiasm, they read to each other the writings of Horace, Bacon, Dryden, and Pope. (Grayson, *Memoir of James L. Petigru*, 42-44).

Grayson taught at Beaufort and Savannah; studied law; edited the Beaufort *Gazette;* and as a strong advocate of Nullification served ten years in the South Carolina Legislature. He also represented the Beaufort district in Congress (1833-37) and was Collector of Customs of the Port of Charleston, 1841-53. In this period Grayson changed his political ideas and became a strong opponent of secession, presenting his beliefs through numerous pamphlets. The most notable of these, strongly influenced in manner of argument by Jonathan Swift, are the *Letters of Curtius*. After being removed as Collector, Grayson purchased the Fair Lawn Plantation near Charleston, thus following "the approved Custom in closing every kind of a career" (*Petigru*, 136).

Since he felt that "my calling had left me," he began writing poems and essays. In 1854, he published *The Hireling and the Slave*, a book-length attack on the inhumanity of industrialism and defence of the humaneness of slavery. But Grayson had thrown the argument into poetry not merely "to diversify the mode, if not the matter, of the argument;" he sought, also, to offer "some variety to the poetic forms that are almost universally prevalent" by returning to the "School of Dryden and Pope." (*The Hireling and the Slave*, 1854, p. xv). Although his work received more praise for its didactic than for its poetic qualities, Grayson was quickly

172

accepted as one of the Charleston literary coterie. A frequenter of Russell's Bookshop, he was on intimate terms with Simms, Petigru, Dickson, Bruns, Hayne, and Timrod. When this group started *Russell's Magazine* in 1857, Grayson took an active part as a sub-editor and regular contributor. A lover of argument, he debated fiercely with S. Henry Dickson in *Russell's* on the subject of duelling, and his attack on romantic poetry so excited Timrod that he immediately prepared an answering essay.

In his unpublished autobiography,* Grayson presents in a slightly different form most of the arguments in "What is Poetry?" He felt that Coleridge beclouded every issue that he touched, and that Wordsworth's mechanical use of nature, Shelley's metaphysical sentiments, Keats's "renovated pagan deities," and Southey's Hindu "mythological monsters" all led to a "transcendental oracular school" of poetry and criticism. Grayson's allegiance was elsewhere: "My select friends are not of the new schools. I adhere to the old masters and their followers. I believe in Dryden and Pope . . . I have faith in the ancient classical models, the masters directly or indirectly of all the great poets of modern times . . . The sin of modern poetry consists in exaggeration of sentiment, of passion, of description, of every thing. It wants simplicity and truth. It seeks to be sublime and becomes inflated. It strives to be deep and is obscure only. It strains after the new and the wonderful and sinks into the grotesque and unintelligible. The modern poet finds the field of thought occupied and is driven to shifts and expedients." (122-23, 247-48).

Grayson thought of himself as an advocate of common sense, a follower in criticism of Samuel Johnson. He had no patience with theories of inspiration: the poet is simply "a very pains taking individual and works as hard at his trade as any other intellectual laborer . . . He toils after thoughts, words, and images. Sometimes they come readily. Sometimes they refuse to come at all. His tools are pen and ink. His inspiration is the same as that of every other mental workman, the excitement of thought." (135; 275). With equal vigor, Grayson objected to the idea that poets are a mysterious race of a particular moral nature different from the rest of mankind, and thus not amenable to the same judgments. Poets have a diversity and peculiarity of temperament common to men, not because they are poets but because they are men: "It would be as rational, perhaps more so, to ascribe Byron's licentiousness to his deformed foot than to his genius for poetry." (139, 283). He thought that the greatest of English poets— Chaucer, Spenser, Shakspere, and Milton—were men of moral character,

* Manuscript, *The Autobiography of William J. Grayson*, written in 1863; typescript edited by Robert Duncan Bass, 1933; both in the South Caroliniana Collection, University of South Carolina Library. The first page number is to the manuscript; the second to Bass's edition. Practically all of Grayson's remarks on literature are in Ch. XI.

but he was also positive that the best verse did not excuse evil: "The best songs are the crackling of thorns under a pot compared with the interests of truth and virtue." (140, 285-6).

In his autobiography, Grayson drily remarks about Timrod's response to his charge that Wordsworth was mechanical in his enthusiasm: "I said so once and was nearly annihilated by an indignant admirer who over-whelmed me with quotations to prove how much I was in error. The quota-tions did not change my opinions." (Unnumbered leaf between 124 and 125; 251-2).

Grayson's mind was dogmatic, but it was evidently stimulating. He enjoyed writing, and he had a salty, apt command of metaphor that makes his prose readable and diverting. In addition to his essays and numerous short poems, he wrote two other long poems, *The Country* (1858) and *Marion* (1860). During the War he wrote, also, the *Memoir of James L. Petigru*, which was not published until 1866; and his autobiography, which has not been published. He died at Newberry, South Carolina, on Oct. 4, 1863.

I have retained all of Grayson's individualities of style, including some errors that were undoubtedly caused by bad printing and proof-reading. The obvious mistakes in the text that I have corrected are: ¶2, discription: description; ¶4, Poets invokes: Poet invokes; ¶5, a superfluous quotation mark after the word immortality; ¶11, on the poetry: in the poetry; ¶16, kingsman's: kinsman's; ¶23, it's sides: its sides.

[2] In the *Biographia Literaria*, Ch. I, Coleridge describes the poetic training given him at Christ's Hospital under "a very severe master, the Reverend James Bowyer." Bowyer (or Boyer) emphasized the logic in poetry, and abominated trite and inexact phrasing. Coleridge notes: "*Lute, harp*, and *lyre, Muse, Muses*, and *inspiration, Pegasus, Parnassus*, and *Hip-picrene* were all an abomination to him. In fancy I can almost hear him now, exclaiming 'Harp? Harp? Lyre? pen and ink, boy, you mean! Muse, boy, Muse? Your nurse's daughter, you mean! Pierian spring? Oh aye! the cloister-pump, I suppose!' " For other tributes to Bowyer, see Coleridge's *Table Talk*, Aug. 16, 1832, and Charles Lamb's essay, "Christ's Hospital Five-and-Thirty Years Ago."

[3] Horace, "odi profanum volgus et arceo," *Carm.* 3.1.1. The phrases in the preceding paragraph may have been suggested by Horace, especially the "non usitata nec tenui ferar / penna," *Carm.* 2.20.2. The phrase "favete linguis" is also from Horace, *Carm.* 3.1.2.

[4] Cicero, *Pro Archia*. Grayson paraphrases rather than translates, but he gives the exact meaning of the passage, and gives also an accurate summary of the remainder of the oration.

[5] John Selden (1584-1654) in his *History of Tythes* (1618) gave offence

to the clergy, and the book was suppressed by public authority. His many works were collected by Dr. David Wilkins.

6 Evidently a misprint. James Hannay (1827-73), English essayist and novelist, wrote *Satire and Satirists* (1854).

7 William Lisle Bowles (1762-1850) edited the works of Pope (1806) and his unfavorable comments and his critical theory roused a critical furore that lasted into the 1820's. Bowles wrote that images and thoughts derived from nature and the passions were always superior to those derived from art and manners; therefore, Pope was an inferior poet. Many writers defended Pope against Bowles; most notably, Byron in a *Letter to John Murray*. The Wordsworth reference is to the "Observations Prefixed to 'Lyrical Ballads'" (1800).

8 In a letter from Wordsworth to an English friend, John Wilson (Christopher North), June, 1802, in *The Early Letters of William and Dorothy Wordsworth* (1787-1805), edited by Ernest de Selincourt, pp. 292-98.

9 *Ibid.*

10 Addison in two *Spectator* papers (#70, May 21, 1711, and #74, May 25, 1711) discussed the ballad form, using "Chevy Chase" as an example. Percy's *Reliques of Ancient English Poetry* gives a very long, ancient version. The two lines below do not appear in Addison's discussion; Percy in Part II, ll. 121-2:

> For when both his leggis wear hewyne in to,
> Yet he knyled and fought on hys kne.

Chace was a variant spelling, and the original form was probably Cheviat.

11 In his *Life of Johnson*, Oxford Edition, 1904, II: 121-22, Sept. 18, 1777, Boswell related the story and quotes the poem. Johnson is here referring to imitation rather than to ballads: "He [Johnson] observed, that a gentleman of eminence in literature had got into a bad style of poetry of late. 'He puts (said he,) a very common thing in a strange dress till he does not know it himself, and thinks other people do not know it.' *Boswell.* 'That is owing to his being so much versant in old English poetry.' *Johnson.* 'What is that to the purpose, Sir? If I say a man is drunk, and you tell me it is owing to his taking much drink, the matter is not mended.'"

12 Perhaps Coleridge's most striking statement of *good sense* in poetry (not common sense) comes at the end of Ch. XIV of the *Biographia Literaria*: "Finally, *Good Sense* is the *Body* of poetic genius, *fancy* its *drapery, Motion* its *life,* and *imagination* the *soul* that is every where, and in each; and forms all into one graceful and intelligent whole." See also Ch. XVIII. Wordsworth in his "Observations Prefixed to 'Lyrical Ballads'" says that his practice of honest description and natural diction must have some worth, "as it is friendly to one property of all good poetry, namely, good sense."

Grayson's spelling of *Marinere* deviates from Coleridge's practice, as well as ordinary usage. It may be intended to suggest a ballad quality, or an archaic form.

¹³ Samuel Johnson's *The Vanity of Human Wishes* (1749). Scott, writing about Samuel Johnson in his *Lives of Eminent Novelists and Dramatists* (p. 501 of 1887 ed., Chandos Classics), makes a more general statement: "The 'Vanity of Human Wishes,' the deep and pathetic morality of which has often extracted tears from those whose eyes wander dry over pages professedly sentimental."

¹⁴ Coleridge, *Biographia Literaria*, Ch. I.

¹⁵ From Wordsworth, "Milton! thou shouldst be living at this hour." The line reads: "Thy soul was like a Star, and dwelt apart."

¹⁶ See Coleridge's *Biographia Literaria*, Ch. IV, and the first half of Ch. XXII. On the preference for Collins over Gray, see Ch. I.

¹⁷ *Ibid.*, Ch. XXII.

¹⁸ Lancelot Brown (1715-1783), known as "Capability Brown," revived the natural style of landscape-gardening, and laid out the gardens at Kew and Blenheim.

¹⁹ Originally written by Pope, "Epistle to Dr. Arbuthnot," l. 339:

> And thought a lie in verse or prose the same.
> That not in fancy's maze he wander'd long,
> But stooped to truth, and moralized his song

Byron, "Letter to John Murray, Esq., on the Rev. W. L. Bowles's Strictures on the Life and Writings of Pope," in *The Works of Lord Byron*, London, 1832, VI: 369.

²⁰ Coleridge, *Table Talk*, July 12, 1827. See note 8, Timrod's "What is Poetry?"

²¹ Pope, *Imitations of Horace*: Epistles, Book II, Epistle 1, l. 103: "And God the Father turns a school-divine."

²² This high praise of Horace is by Petronius, *Satyricon*, Ch. CXVIII.

INDEX

Addison, Joseph, 141, 175
"Address Delivered at the Opening of the New Theatre at Richmond," 21n, 44n
Advancement of Learning, 48n, 138, 170
Aeschylus, 52
"Aglaus," 56
"Alastor," 6-9
Aldrich, T. B., 20, 49n
American Studies in Honor of William Kenneth Boyd, 27n, 160
Americanism in literature, 28-29, 87-88
Anacreontea, 54n, 66
"Ancient Mariner, The," 78, 142-3, 144, 175-6
"Ante-Bellum Charleston," 59n
Antony and Cleopatra, 89, 159, 168
Appomattox, 44n
Archias, 137, 174
"Arctic Voyager, The," 38
Aristotle, 13, 139
Arnold, Matthew, 48, 66, 120, 130, 157, 170
"Arsenal Hill," 31
"Astrophel," 44
Atlantic Monthly, 49n, 166
Austin, Henry, 52n, 53n, 165-6
Autobiography of William J. Grayson, The, 173
Autographic Relics, 42, 43n

Bacon, Francis, 48, 121, 138, 170, 172
Ballads, 141-42, 175-76
Bass, Robert Duncan, 173
Beauchampe, 46n
Beauties of Shakspear, The, 167
Beauty in poetry, 5, 16-18, 25, 35-38, 76-77, 114-21, 123, 125, 129

Beulah, 51n
Bible, The, 47-8, 71, 149
Billings, Josh, 49n
Biographia Literaria, 158, 159, 163, 164, 167, 170, 174, 175, 176
Blackwood's, 49n
Blair, Hugh, 85, 141, 161
Bookman, The, 52n
Books We Have Made, 41n
Boston, 27, 49n, 97, 166
Boswell, James, 142, 175
Bowles, William Lisle, 139, 151, 175, 176
Bowyer, James, 136, 174
"Boy of Winandermere, The," 81
"Break, Break, Break," 39
Brevity, 16-18, 67-68, 77, 105-07, 111-112, 121-22
Bride of Lammermoor, The, 92
Brontë, Charlotte, 49
Brown, Lancelot, 146, 176
Browning, Elizabeth Barrett, 41, 130
Browning, Robert, 41, 130-1
Bruns, John Dickson, 20, 59, 173
Bruns, Peirce, 9n, 33n, 54n
Bryan, J. P. K., 4n, 32n, 52
Buchanan, Robert, 50, 52
Burke, Edmund, 71, 100, 149, 153
"Burial of Sir John Moore after Corunna," 43n
Burns, Robert, 44, 62, 146
Byron, George Gordon, 7, 33, 42, 58, 88, 121, 125, 128, 143, 147, 167, 173, 175, 176

Calculus, 92
Caldwell, H. H., 160
"Call to Arms, A," 47n
Campbell, Thomas, 57n

177

Cardwell, Guy A. Jr., 6n, 22n, 24n, 42n, 53n, 56n
Carew, Thomas, 82
Carlyle, Thomas, 48n
Castle of Indolence, 42, 163
Catullus, 32, 40, 52-5, 57
Cavalier poetry, 46-47, 57-58n
Century, The, 165
"Character and Scope of the Sonnet, The," 10, 12-13, 25n, 42n, 44n, 61-8, 168. Notes: 157
Charleston, 31n, 38, 39n, 57, 58, 59, 172, 173
Charleston Book, The, 58
Charleston Daily Courier, 47n
Charleston Library Society, 57
Charleston News and Courier, 41n, 59n
Chaucer, Geoffrey, 43, 173
"Chevy Chace," 141-2, 175
Childe Harold's Pilgrimage, 167
Christ, 46
"Christmas," 26
"Christ's Hospital Five-and-Thirty Years Ago," 174
Churchill, Charles, 139
"Churchyard among the Mountains, A," 127
Cicero, 54n, 174
Civil War, 3, 10-11, 26-27, 29-31, 38, 49-50, 60, 161-64, 168-70, 174
"Cloud," 9n
"Clym of the Clough," 140
Coleridge, Samuel Taylor, 14, 48, 69, 73, 76, 77, 78, 80-1, 94, 112, 123, 124, 136, 142, 143, 144, 145, 146, 150, 153, 158, 159, 163, 164, 167, 170, 173, 174, 175, 176
Collins, Wilkie, 48n
Collins, William, 144, 176
Columbia, S. C., 20n, 29n, 31n
Columbiad, 112, 167
"Comus," 71, 149, 153
Conceit, the, 46-47
"Confederates in the Field, The," 21n
Confederacy, 30, 163-4, 169

Confederacy, Atlanta, 168
Contemplation, 7, 24, 35-38, 80, 158, 168-70
Cooke, Philip Pendleton, 97
Copse Hill, 41n, 51
Cornelius Nepos, 55
"Corsair, The," 121
"Cotton Boll, The," 26n, 40, 163
Country, The, 174
Courant, The, 160
Course of Time, The, 99, 164
Courtenay, W. A., 40n, 53, 59n, 165
Cowley, Abraham, 44
Cowper, William, 33, 124
"Culprit Fay, The," 86
"Curse of Kehama," 144

Daily South Carolinian, 19-20, 29n, 31n, 43n, 44n, 48n, 58, 160-1, 161-3, 163-4, 168-9
"Danish Boy," 81
Dante, 16, 17, 105, 112
Dargan, Clara, 49n
Davidson, James Wood, 21, 41, 46, 55, 56n
"Day-Dream, The," 170
De Quincey, Thomas, 124
De Vere, Aubrey, 48, 157
"Death reigns triumphant," 45
"Dedication, A," 34n, 45n, 53n, 54n
"Defence of Poetry, A," 9-10, 158, 167
Defoe, Daniel, 71, 149
Dekker, Thomas, 46
della Torre, John, 59
Dennis, John, 46
"Detached Thoughts on Books and Reading," 167
Dickens, Charles, 48n, 49n, 71, 98, 149, 164
Dickson, S. Henry, 59, 173
Diction, 14-16, 21, 71, 74-76, 122, 148-54, 159, 174, 175
Dimroth, 56
Divine Comedy, 17, 112
Dodd, William, 167
"Dramatic Fragment, A," 33n, 35n, 39, 41n

"Dream, A," 57n
"Dream of Fair Women," 40n
Dreams, 4-5, 7-9, 22, 23, 42-43
"Dreams," 24n
Dryden, John, 33, 124, 139, 172, 173

Editorials by Timrod (quoted), 18-20, 29-31, 41n, 43, 44, 49n, 160-64, 168-70
"Edwin and Angelina," 142
"Elegy in a Country Churchyard," 140, 141, 144
Elements of Criticism, 161
Ennius, 137
Epicurus, 151
"Epistle to Dr. Arbuthnot," 176
Essays (Bacon), 48n
Essays of Elia, 159
"Ethnogenesis," 163
Euclid, 92
Euphony, 21, 122
"Euterpe," 40n
Evans, Augusta, see Wilson, Augusta Evans
Excursion, The, 81, 121, 126, 127, 144, 159, 170

Faërie Queene, 17, 112
Fancy, 11, 25n, 71, 73, 88, 94-95, 118, 148-49, 168, 175
"First Eclogue," 53n
Fielding, Henry, 71, 149
Fiction, 4, 49, 50-52, 71, 87-89, 91-92, 95-96, 105, 149, 160, 161-62
Fidler, William, 33n, 36n
"Field Flowers," 43n, 44n
Flash, Harry Lyndon, 20
Fletcher, John, 46n, 52
Fontaine, F. G. De, 20n, 29n, 31n, 50
"For high honours," 54n
Ford, John, 46n, 52
French, 21, 53n, 55, 56-7
Froissart Ballads, 97
Fusiliers, German, 56, 57

Genesis, 149
German, 53n, 56, 101, 143

German Friendly Society, 57
Gibbes, R. W., 29n
Gildersleeve, Basil, 59
Goethe, Wolfgang, 56
Goldsmith, Oliver, 87, 100, 142
Goodwin, Edith, 46n
Goodwin, Emily Timrod, 18n, 25n, 36n, 39n, 41n, 45n, 46n, 49n, 52, 56n, 58n
Gray, Thomas, 140, 144, 176
Grayson, William J., 13-16, 59, 69-72, 133-54, 158, 166, 172-6
Greek, 21, 53n, 54, 56, 137

Hall, Basil, 98, 164
Hallam, Arthur Henry, 48, 74, 158
"Hark to the Shouting Wind," 39
Hayne, P. H., 4, 12, 20, 21, 25n, 29n, 31, 32, 33n, 36n, 39, 41n, 42n, 43, 44n, 45, 46, 47n, 48, 49, 50, 51-2, 55, 56n, 57n, 58n, 59, 160, 173
Hannay, James, 139, 175
Hebrew literature, 47-8
Henry IV, 160
Henry Timrod, 52n, 53n
Henry Timrod: Man and Poet, 6n, 53n
Herbert, George, 49n
Herodotus, 40
Heustis, Rachel Lyons, see Lyons, Rachel
Hireling and the Slave, The, 172
History, 27-31, 90-91, 95-96, 160, 161-62, 163-64, 168-70
"Hohenlinden," 57n
Holmes, Oliver Wendell, 49n
Home, Henry, 161
Homer, 56, 112, 136, 152-3
Honest Whore, The, 46
Horace, 52, 54n, 55, 57n, 86, 136, 139, 148, 153, 172, 174, 176
Hubbell, Jay B., 9n, 20n, 27n, 29n, 31n, 37n, 41n, 44n, 46n, 160
Hume, David, 96
Hunt, Leigh, 54n, 168
"Hymn of the Nativity," 127

"Idiot Boy," 140, 144
Iliad, 71, 112, 149, 152
Imagination, 7, 10-11, 13, 15, 19, 21, 28, 32, 35, 61, 64, 71, 73-76, 80-81, 88, 90, 94-95, 99, 110-11, 114, 117-20, 124, 131, 147-49, 151-52, 158, 161-62, 167, 168-69, 175
Imagination and Fancy, 168
Imitations of Horace, 176
"Imperfect Sympathies," 159
Improvisations, 12, 65-66, 119, 142, 168-69
"In Bowers of Ease," 43n
"In Memoriam," 39, 40n, 121
Independent, The, 165
Ingelow, Jean, 41n, 50, 52
Inspiration, 4-5, 7, 9, 10-12, 17-18, 19, 21, 30, 32-38, 64-66, 89-90, 118-20, 135-37, 162, 164, 167, 168-70, 173
"Intimations of Immortality from Recollections of Early Childhood," 33n, 81, 127
Intuition, 4-5, 6, 7, 9, 10, 21, 23-24, 34-38, 113-14, 135-37
"It is a beauteous evening, calm and free," 81
Ivanhoe, 71, 72, 96, 149

Jane Eyre, 49
Johnson, Samuel, 14, 100, 140, 141, 153, 173, 175, 176
Joscelyn, 51n
Juvenal, 139, 140, 148

Kames, Lord, 85, 161
"Katie," 33
Keats, John, 5, 41-2, 42n, 173
King John, 45-6

"La Belle Juive," 47n
La Nouvelle Héloïse, 56
Lamartine, 49n
Lamb, Charles, 48, 78, 107, 159, 167, 174
Language, 14-16, 17-18, 21, 33, 54, 71-72, 74-76, 114, 122, 143, 150-54, 159, 174

"Laodamia," 62, 81, 158
Last Essays of Elia, 167
Last Years of Henry Timrod, The, cited frequently in footnotes to Introduction, 160
"Late Henry Timrod, The," 37n
Latin, 52-56, 59n
LeConte, Joseph, 13-14
Lectures on Rhetoric and Belles-Lettres, 85, 161
Legaré, Hugh Swinton, 59
Legaré, James Mathewes, 59
"Let V——y prattle," 54n
"Letter to John Murray," 175, 176
"Letter to Samuel Hartlib: On Education," 158
Letters of Curtius, 172
Lewisohn, Ludwig, 41n
"Lines," 38n
"Lines to R. L.," 38
"Literary Nationalism in the Old South," 27n, 160
"Literary pranks," 31
Literary Remains, 158
"Literature in the South," 19n, 27-29, 83-102. Notes: 160-4
"Little Spot of Dingy Earth, A," 22n
Lloyd, Mrs. Kate Timrod, 40, 53, 165
Local Color, 28-30, 42n, 58n, 87-89, 161-62
Locksley Hall, 39
"London," 141
Longfellow, Henry W., 86
Longinus, 54n
"Love's Philosophy," 9n
Lucretius, 77, 151
Lyons, Rachel, 30n, 33n, 36, 47n, 50n, 51n, 59n

Macaulay, T. B., 124
Mackay, Charles, 97
"Madoc," 144
Marryatt, Frederick, 98, 160, 164
Marvell, Andrew, 46
"Maryland, My Maryland," 30, 163
"Maud," 38n, 40n, 144

"Madeline," 47n
Marion, 174
"Marseillaise Hymn," 170
Martial, 53n, 55
Matter-of-factness in poetry, 16, 78, 80-81, 123, 145-46, 159, 174
Maynard, François, 55
McCarter, James, 57n
Memorabilia and Anecdotal Reminiscences of Columbia, S. C., 31n
Memoir of James L. Petigru, 172, 174
Memories of the Timrod Revival, 40n, 53n, 59n, 165
Messiah, The, 143
Metamorphoses, 55
Metaphysical poetry, 46-47
"Methought I saw the Footsteps of a Throne," 81
Metre, 14, 15, 39, 56, 69, 72, 74-77, 104, 113, 122, 149-53, 158, 159
Middleton, Thomas, 46
Milton, John, 14, 32, 33, 35, 39, 40, 45, 62, 63, 71, 76, 77, 107 112, 115, 121, 122, 124, 127, 136, 143, 149-50, 151, 153, 157, 158, 167, 173, 176
Modern Painters, 159
Moore, Thomas, 42, 58, 61, 62, 66, 82, 128, 158
"Morality," 157, 170
"Mother," 140
"Mother's Wail, A," 26-7, 56n
"My Last Duchess," 41
Mycerinus, 40n

"Names of the Months Phonetically Expressive," 44n
Napoleon, 141
"National Songs," 30, 163-64
"Nationality in Literature," 29n, 161-63
Nature, 7, 9, 10-11, 26-7, 32-8, 43, 44, 49, 57, 79-81, 99, 115-19, 121, 124-28, 131, 138, 140-43, 145-47, 158, 161-62, 169, 173, 175, 176

Neo-classicism, 13, 22, 28, 33, 85-6, 98, 99, 104-5, 123-5, 139-41, 172-3, 175, 176
Never Too Late to Mend?, 52
New York, 27, 97
"Night Piece, A," 81
"Noon. An Eclogue," 58n
North American Review, The, 93
Novum Organum, 48n

"Observations Prefixed to 'Lyrical Ballads,'" 157, 158, 159, 167, 170, 175
"Ode," 27
"OEnone," 38n, 40n
"On the Nature and Uses of Art," 14n
Oratory, 137-8, 152-53, 174
Ossian, 141
"Out upon it!", 54n
Outlines of Natural Philosophy, 163
Outlook, The, 157
Ovid, 49, 55

Page, Walter Hines, 9n, 56n
"Palace of Art, The," 40n
Paradise Lost, 17, 40, 71, 99, 106, 107-13, 121, 143, 149, 152, 157, 164, 167, 168, 169
"Past, The," 52n
Percy, Thomas, 175
Persius, 40, 55-56
Personal Talk, 170
Petigru, James L., 59, 172, 173
Petronius, 176
"Philip, My Son," 49n
Philip Van Artevelde, 164
Philosophy, 7-9, 18, 35, 37-38, 51n, 67, 69-70, 77, 80, 85, 92, 94-95, 99, 100, 104, 110-11, 113, 120-22, 124-27, 130, 137-39, 149, 151-52, 161, 170, 173
"Philosophy of Composition, The," 168
Phoenix, The, 31n
Plato, 137
Playfair, John, 92, 163

Poe, Edgar Allan, 16-17, 21, 39, 96, 105-07, 111-13, 114-16, 119, 120, 121, 122, 123, 125, 129, 130, 166, 167, 168

Poems (Timrod), 160

Poems of Henry Timrod (Hayne ed.), frequently cited in footnotes to Introduction

Poems of Henry Timrod (Memorial ed.), frequently cited in footnotes to Introduction

Poems of the Imagination, 170

"Poems on the Naming of Places, IV," 159

Poems on Various Subjects, 57-58

"Poet! if on a lasting fame be bent," 34

Poetasters, 18-20, 62, 66, 96-97, 153, 163

Poetic diction, 14-16, 21, 71, 74-76

"Poetic Principle, The," 105ff., 167

Poetic prose, 14, 16, 69-78, 112-13, 138, 148-54, 159

"Poet's Epitaph, A," 81, 168

Pollok, Robert, 164

Pomponius, 55n

Pope, Alexander, 28, 33, 85, 86, 87, 99, 124, 140, 141, 172, 173, 175, 176

Power in poetry, 18, 25, 117-18

"Præceptor Amat," 41, 52n, 56

"Prelude," 127, 144, 157, 168, 170

"Princess, The," 40n, 88, 170

Propertius, 54n, 55

"Prose and Song," 76-77, 159

"Quebec," 57n

Rabelais, 172

Randall, James Ryder, 20

"Rape of the Lock, The," 141

"Rationale of Poetry, The," 165

"Raven, The," 119, 120

Reade, Charles, 52

Reading (Timrod's), 32-60

Recollections of the Table-Talk of Samuel Rogers, 157

Religion and poetry, 5, 42n, 47-48, 107-10, 121, 127, 130, 136-37, 167

Reliques of Ancient English Poetry, 175

Remains in Prose and Verse of Arthur Henry Hallam, 158

"Reminiscence of Henry Timrod, A," 59n

Requier, A. J., 20

"Retirement," 24

Reynolds, Sir Joshua, 100

"Rhapsody of a Southern Winter Night, A," 22n, 24n, 39

Robinson, Felicia, 52n

Robinson Crusoe, 71, 149

Rogers, Samuel, 12n, 62-63, 143, 157

Rousseau, 56-57

"Rule Britannia," 30, 163

Russell, John, 59

Russell's Magazine, 38n, 42n, 48, 69, 70, 78, 157, 158, 160, 172, 173

Sappho, 54n

Satire, 98, 100, 139, 147-48, 175

Satires, 207n, 209-10

Satyricon, 176

Science, 14, 92-94, 117, 123, 158, 159

Scott, Walter, 29, 71, 87-88, 89, 96, 105, 140, 143, 149, 161, 176

Selby, Julian A., 31n

Selden, John, 138, 174

Seminole War, 56

Sensibility, 4-5, 11, 15, 42n, 70, 73-74

Shakspere, William, 14, 29, 33, 43n, 44-46, 83, 89, 99, 109, 124, 128, 143, 153, 159, 160, 161, 162, 167, 168, 173

"Shakspeare, with introductory matter on Poetry, the Drama, and the Stage," 158

Shelley, Percy Bysshe, 6-10, 33n, 41, 158, 167, 173

"She was a phantom of delight," 128-29

Shirley, 49

Simile, Miltonic, 40

Simms, W. G., 18n, 19n, 20, 31n, 33n, 37-38, 45, 46, 51, 53n, 56, 58, 59, 96, 160-61, 173

Simonides, 56n

"Six months's such a wonderful time," 54n

Smith, Adam, 140

Smith, Sidney, 49n

Snowden, Yates, 59n

"Song/Air—The Glasses Sparkle on the Board," 58n

"Song" ("The Zephyr that toys with thy curls"), 9n

"Song at the Feast of Brougham Castle," 81

"Song of Mignon," 56

"Song—When I bade thee adieu," 42n

Songs, national, 30, 163-64, 169-70

Sonnet, 11-13, 24, 61-68, 157

"Sonnet—In the Deep Shadow," 24n

"Sonnet IV—They dub thee idler, smiling sneeringly," 24n

"Sonnet V—Some truths there be are better left unsaid," 24n

"Sonnet X," 25n

"Sonnet XI," 46n

"Sonnet XIV—Are these wild thoughts, thus fettered in my rhymes," 24n

Sophocles, 52

"Sorrow," 157

Southern Bivouac, The, 59n

"Southern Literature," 29n, 162-63

Southern Literary Messenger, 30n, 33n, 47n, 48, 51n, 52n

Southern nationalism, 27-31, 83-102, 130, 160-64

"Southern Nationality," 29n

Southern Review, The, 59

Southern Society, 37n, 53n, 58n

Southey, Robert, 173

Spenser, Edmund, 17, 43-44, 112, 173

"Spring," 26n

Statius, 55

Sterling, John, 48, 76-77, 159

St. Elmo, 50-51

"Star-Spangled Banner, The," 30, 163

Sublimity, 17, 105-6, 108, 110-11, 113, 116, 149, 163-64, 173

Suckling, John, 47, 54n

"Sullivan's Island," 58n

"Summer Bower, The," 36-37, 39

"Summer Shower, A," 9n

"Sweet let not our slanderers," 53n

Swift, Jonathan, 172

Swinburne, Algernon, 50

Sybilline Leaves, 170

Table Talk, 159, 176

"Talking Oak," 21

Taylor, Henry, 48, 95, 164

Taylor, Jeremy, 76

Tennyson, Alfred, 21, 32, 33, 38-40, 49n, 86, 115, 119-20, 121, 122, 128, 129, 131, 144, 166, 170

Thackeray, W. M., 48n

"Thalaba," 144

"Theory of Poetry, A," 6, 10, 16-18, 22n, 25n, 29n, 33n, 35n, 39, 40, 41, 43n, 44n, 48n, 103-32, 159. Notes: 165-71

"There is I know not what about thee," 53n

Thompson, H. T., 52n, 53n

Thomson, James, 33, 42-43, 90, 124, 160, 166

"Thorn," 140, 141

"Three years she grew in sun and shower," 81

Tibullus, 54n, 55

Timrod-Goodwin Collection, 18n, 25n, 36n, 39n, 41n, 45n, 46n, 49n, 51n, 52n, 56n

"Timrod's Essays in Literary Criticism," 10n

Timrod, William Henry, 25n, 36n, 45, 56, 57-58

"Tintern Abbey, Lines on," 79-80, 121, 125-26, 159, 170
"To Anna," 25n
"To Harry," 57n
"To his Coy Mistress," 46
"To our Poetical Contributors" (quoted), 19-20
"To Pyrrha," 57n
"To William Wordsworth," 170
Tom Jones, 71, 95, 149
Tooker, L. Frank, 42n
"Tractate on Education," 71, 77, 149-50, 158
Trent, W. P., 18n, 31n, 33n, 160
"Troubles of a Midsummer Night," 31
Truth in poetry, 5, 6, 7, 18, 23, 25, 35-38, 68, 94-95, 117-18, 120, 123-28, 130, 131-32, 170, 173, 174, 176
Tupper, M. F., 96
"Two Field Flowers," 44n
"Two Voices," 166

"Ulysses," 38, 88
Uncollected Poems of Henry Timrod, cited frequently in notes to Introduction
Unity, 13, 16-18, 63-64, 67-68, 77, 106-14, 120, 122-23, 127, 143, 151-52, 159, 175
"Unpublished Letters of Henry Timrod," 33n, 36n

"Vanity of Human Wishes," 143, 176
"Venus and Adonis," 44
Vergil, 52, 53n, 140, 141, 153
Villette, 49
"Vision of Poesy, A," 4-11, 22n, 25n, 26n, 34, 35n, 42n, 44
Voigt, G. P., 10n
Voltaire, 143
"Vox et Præterea Nihil," 24n

"War and Literature," 31n, 168-69
War, Civil, 3, 10-11, 26-27, 29-31, 38, 49-50, 60, 161-64, 168-70, 174
Ward, Artemus, 49n
Wauchope, G. A., 6n, 53n
"Westminster Bridge," 81
"What is Poetry?" (Grayson), 13-16, 68-72, 133-54, 166. Notes: 172-76
"What is Poetry?" (Timrod), 10, 11, 13-16, 69-82, 167. Notes: 158-59
"White Doe of Rylestone," 144
Whittier, John G., 20, 49n, 52n
"Why Silent," 23n, 25n
Wilhelm Meister, 56
William Gilmore Simms, 18n, 31n, 33n, 160
"William Henry Timrod, the Charleston Volunteers, and the Defense of St. Augustine," 56n
Wilson, Augusta Evans, 50-51
Wilson, John (Christopher North), 175
"Windsor Forest," 124
Wolfe, Charles, 43n
Wolfe, Gen. James, 144
Words, 14-16, 17-18, 21, 33, 54, 71-72, 74-76, 114, 122, 143, 150-54, 159, 173, 175
Wordsworth, William, 7, 9n, 12, 16, 28, 32-36, 39, 40, 41, 52, 62, 63, 66, 67, 78, 79-82, 86, 87, 90, 99, 117, 121, 123, 124-29, 132, 139-40, 141, 143, 144-47, 157, 158, 159, 167, 168, 170, 173, 174, 175, 176
"World is too much with us, The," 81

"Yew Trees," 81
"Youth and Manhood," 22-23

www.ingramcontent.com/pod-product-compliance
Lightning Source LLC
Chambersburg PA
CBHW030546030726
47495CB00004B/1154